0717 117

D1134321

* Dub. Collection *

* 'Hold at Desk*

DUBLIN CHURCHES

Building a Dublin church,
wood cut from *Holinshed's Chronicles of Ireland*

Peter Costello

Dublin Churches

*'In my father's house
there are many mansions.'*
John, 14:2

Gill and Macmillan

Published in Ireland by
Gill and Macmillan Ltd
Goldenbridge
Dublin 8
with associated companies in Auckland, Delhi, Gaborone, Hamburg, Harare,
Hong Kong, Johannesburg, Kuala Lumpur, Lagos, London,
Manzini, Melbourne, Mexico City, Nairobi,
New York, Singapore, Tokyo
© Peter Costello 1989
Print origination by Keystrokes Ltd, Dublin
Printed by The Bath Press, Bath

All rights reserved. No part of this publication may be copied,
reproduced or transmitted in any form or by any means,
without permission of the publishers.

LEABHARLANNA ATHA CLIATH
BALLYFERMOT LIBRARY
ACC. NO.   0717 117006
COPY NO.   XX 3035
INV NO/90 4634
PRICE IR£   14.98
CLASS Ref 726.5094183

Contents

In memory of John Betjeman,
to whose enthusiasms
I owe so much

Introduction

Dublin is a Christian city. Few streets are out of sight of a church steeple or tower, few homes out of hearing of bells ringing the Angelus or summoning the faithful to Sunday services. Behind these sights and sounds, behind the little girls in their white dresses or the Christmas crib outside the Mansion House, lies 1,500 years of tradition. And because it is Christian, Dublin is a religious city, a city of churches, of chapels, bethels, salems, meeting houses, gospel halls, of synagogues and lately even mosques. In a city famous for its architecture, a city dominated by government and commercial buildings, churches are the only real public buildings, far more so than civic offices or banking houses. They alone are for public use, paid for out of choice by the public for their own use. They are the buildings on which the people's real lives are centred. They reflect in an immediate way their hopes and fears, their feelings about their place in this world, and the next. Churches are the people's architecture. And they have been for 1,500 years.

This book presents only a small sample of the city's places of worship and prayer, perhaps a fifth of the total. In making my choice I have aimed at variety, and as wide a spread as possible of age, location and creed. The churches chosen are also from the real Dublin of today, rather than the historical inner core, from the conurbation that sprawls from Balgriffin south to Bray. Many have been called upon, a few have been chosen. No-one need remind me of what I have neglected to mention: I am only too aware of the fine things that have been left out, and of the things left unsaid. I believe this is the first book to deal with places of worship and prayer from all our traditions, old and new. I hope it will lead to a greater appreciation of a heritage of faith and belief we all share. Today we are only too conscious of what divides us. What unites us needs to be respected too. Our traditional sense of religion can be one of those things.

All traces are now lost of the earliest religious sites in Dublin, those of the pagan Celts. The early Irish venerated high places, fresh-water springs, and clearings in forests. It is likely that such very ancient Christian sites as St Audoen's on the highest street in Dublin, of St Patrick's with its holy well, of St Doulagh's in the cleared plain to the north of the city, have been sacred places since the dawn of Irish history.

Tradition (rather than history) records that Christianity was brought to Dublin by St Patrick in AD 450, as good a date as any in the life of a man about whom we know so little, and from which those 1,500 years are counted. He baptised the local king and some of his people in a well on an island in the River Poddle on which St Patrick's Cathedral now stands. There a small church came to be built in due course. In Christian

Celtic times there was a scattering of a dozen or more little churches or monasteries around Dublin. In the city itself such sites as Cill Cele Chriost, where Christ Church is, St Patrick's, St Kevin's, St Bride's, St Martin's and St Mac Tail's were rebuilt upon into modern times.

Early Dublin did not amount to much more than a small settlement on the ridge above the actual ford of hurdles which gave the place its Gaelic name, and a monastic settlement below it, more or less marked by the circular curve of St Stephen's Street today. This was beside the Black Pool (Dubh Linn) that gave the place its Norse name, Dyflin, when those invaders moored their boats there.

The Norse were pagans. Their sanctuary was on a site in what is now Dame Street; at a later date a church (dedicated to St Andrew) was built there. In the course of time, through cultural contact and intermarriage, the city became Christian and small churches, such as St Olaf's (later the medieval St John's in Fishamble Street) were erected. Sitric Silken Beard, the Norse king of Dublin, founded Christ Church, again on an older site, and St Mary's Abbey in 1032.

The assimilation of the Norse was not complete when the Norman invasion came. The Normans brought their own vigorous and well-connected culture with them. From now on Dublin was a city tied to English and European influences. The old Norse churches were rebuilt in the new modern Norman style, and no doubt there were protests about that, as there have been in all periods when the old has been renewed.

During the Middle Ages the city spread out over the plain below the High Street and into the Coombe. Churches and religious houses were built there, where Trinity stands, and to the south and west. The city then shared a common Christian culture with the island as a whole and with Europe.

This ended with the Reformation and Counter-Reformation. A fatal date in the history of Dublin, because of the division it opened up, was the election of George Browne as Archbishop in January 1536. He was not recognised by the Pope. In Ireland however, unlike other Reformation countries, the Catholic hierarchy was maintained in continuity, with gaps only between 1534 and 1555, 1651, 1680 and 1683. These gaps represent the periods of most intense difficulty for Catholics in the city.

From the point of view of the established Church, Catholics and other Dissenters were all of a kind, to be treated mildly or harshly as the situation demanded. Slowly things improved, first for the independent Protestants, then eventually for the Catholics, until by the beginning of the eighteenth century the Catholic Church was once more openly at work.

This meant that all the older churches are now Church of Ireland churches, as are the public churches of the eighteenth century. Then Catholics and Dissenters had their chapels in back streets, or behind other houses, certainly out of sight of the King's Highway. In Eustace Street on Dublin's left bank were Quaker and

Presbyterian meeting-places, while around Cook Street were numerous Catholic houses, convents and chapels.

All the Catholic chapels of this period have been swept away, though a number of Dissenter places of worship survive. Catholic church building began in the second half of the eighteenth century, but most of what we can see today belongs to the nineteenth century.

From the 1800s on the Church of Ireland began to rebuild older churches and erect new ones, especially in the country around the city. The remarkable work of John Semple belongs to this period. But the great era of Catholic building came after the Synod of Thurles and the advent of Cardinal Cullen. The city witnessed a century of Catholic building that passed through several phases. Here the work of Patrick Byrne is pre-eminent.

It began with churches in the classical style (the Anglicans preferred gothic), then towards the end of the century it moved to a neo-gothic and then a Hiberno-Romanesque style. After the creation of the Free State, seen by many as the triumph of Catholic nationalism, a new series of churches was built in the growing suburbs of Dublin, all of a huge basilica style. This period was to have culminated in the erection of a Catholic cathedral in Merrion Square which was bought for this purpose in the 1920s.

This period ended in the 1950s. The renewals of Vatican II, many of which in their spirit ran quite counter to the feelings of Irish nationalist Catholicism, made themselves felt at the moment when the first churches in a completely modern style with no historical references were being built.

The Catholic churches of today are becoming smaller and cheaper, in recognition of real costs, social, religious and financial. The Catholic churches of the future will, I suspect, be even smaller, more intimate and communal than now.

In this they will be following the Church of Ireland. The Anglican community in Dublin, like the Protestant community as a whole, suffered a major haemorrhage of members in the 1920s. Its survival was in doubt. Even today, on a national scale, numbers are not large. But in Dublin, or more especially in the southern county, no-one who uses his eyes can have any doubts about the health and prosperity of the Church of Ireland. Not only have the parishes grown, they are building schools and halls now, and perhaps eventually new churches. The last Anglican church built in Dublin is, in fact, St Mary's Crumlin, in 1942.

Incidentally, I use 'Anglican' as a synonym for 'Church of Ireland' and not simply as a part of the latter's tradition.

For the smaller communities survival is a different matter. The older Protestant communities, the Presbyterians, Baptists and Quakers, maintain themselves. So too do the Methodists, the Unitarians and the Salvation Army. A sense of reality here too suggests that they will survive.

A feature of modern Dublin has been the appearance of other religious groups.

These include Christian Scientists, Lutherans, Mennonites, Bible Christians and Evangelicals of various kinds, Greek Orthodox and Catholic Traditionalists. And there are the Jews, who have been in Ireland since the seventeenth century, and the Moslems who have just arrived. And for those in search of religious novelty there are Theosophists (with whom Yeats was once involved), Esoteric Buddhists and Tibetan Buddhists, Hare Krishna followers, Latter Day Saints, Seventh Day Adventists and Pentecostalists. All of these have places of their own, a few of which have been included here. What they offer is a religious experience combined with a sense of close social support, which appeals to many individuals in a period when many personal and social ties are breaking down.

'Dublin is a Christian city': is this true still? A major impression left after the research for this book is that it is not. Everywhere we found locked and vandalised churches, Catholic and Protestant. This is no longer for some priests and rectors a matter of surprise, but it was for me. For the malicious, under-employed, poorly educated youth of the city, a church is just another badly protected building to be covered in graffiti, broken into, desecrated, vandalised, burnt down. We found Fascist and Satanic symbols on Coolock's Anglican church, the pledges of young lovers on the doorjambs of Donnycarney Catholic church: such things speak for themselves. They are omens of the future. But not perhaps to those who wish it was 1688 or 1868 or 1932.

This last year was the year of the Eucharistic Congress, the zenith of the Catholic century that ended, as I say, in the 1950s. The decision in 1974 not to build a Catholic cathedral in Merrion Square but to give it back to the people will be recognised as a watershed. Whatever the religious life of the country may develop into, there is no going back, for anyone. It will never be 1688, 1868 or 1932 again. All Christians, all religious people, have more in common with each other than they do with the increasingly secularised and de-Christianised world around them. This will inevitably bring them together in their common interest.

A common problem, which this book will make clear, is the fate of redundant churches. As I write these words the Church of Ireland has announced the closure of twelve churches in Meath. As many as that have already gone in Dublin. A multitude of Dissenting places of architectural interest have gone too or are in danger. So too are several Catholic churches, a fact which only adroit use of resources has hidden. How long will Patrick Byrne's St Paul's on Arran Quay, or St Audoen's in High Street, stay open?

This is not a matter for the Church authorities alone. Churches are a special kind of public rather than private property. To close them is to rip out the fabric of a community. They belong to the community because the community has paid for them. In the case of early Anglican churches, tithes ensured that Catholics also contributed to their building, and so ought to have an interest in their fate.

I began this survey thinking that when a church was redundant a tasteful conversion into something new like offices was the answer. Certainly in Dublin many fine conversions have been done, with skill and taste. Now I am not so sure. When a public building such as a church is converted to private use the whole community suffers a loss.

I now think that the only role for these churches is another form of community use. An example has just come to hand. The Free Church in Great Charles Street, a fine building dating from 1800, now no longer needed by the parish of St Thomas and St George, has been sold to a charity who plan to use it as an education centre for the Travellers. The need to preserve the building has been met by filling an even greater need to an under-privileged section of society.

No more nice offices then. Churches are people's architecture. Let them belong to the people.

I began by saying that churches are the real public buildings of the city. They stand, whatever their denomination, at the centre of a community, larger or smaller as the case may be. They are crucial to the lives of 30,000 people in Donnybrook, or thirty people in the Congregational Chapel in Kilmainham. They combine in a unique way public life with personal devotion. They are the essential part of the city's very nature, and have been for 1,500 years.

Dublin
1989

The Cathedral Church of St Patrick, Patrick Street

[CHURCH OF IRELAND]

Tradition records that when St Patrick on his mission to Ireland reached Dublin he baptised those converting to the new religion at a well on a small island in the River Poddle. The well was discovered during excavations in 1901, and is marked today by a small stone in the park alongside the cathedral.

Here at a later date a Celtic church in wood, dedicated to the Apostle of Ireland, was built. The present cathedral, however, dates from Norman times.

The structure owes its origins to John Comyn, who altered the monastic nature of Christ Church Cathedral, but as Archbishop wished to be beyond the control of the city. He built a palace outside the city (now Kevin Street police station), and began the new church of St Patrick which was dedicated on St Patrick's Day, 1192. The church was raised to the status of a cathedral by Henry de Loundres in 1216. He rebuilt the cathedral on a larger scale, rededicating it in 1254. The Lady Chapel was completed in 1270. Fire destroyed the tower in 1362, and it was rebuilt by Archbishop Minot in 1370 as the tallest in these islands. The steeple, which is by far the most striking feature of the church, was erected only in the eighteenth century.

The confusion about the two cathedrals was not finally resolved until 1872, when St Patrick's was made a national cathedral in which all the dioceses of Ireland were represented, whilst Christ Church became the cathedral of Dublin alone.

In the centuries after the Reformation the fabric of the cathedral decayed. In the 1850s Dean Pakenham restored the Lady Chapel. But work on the main fabric had to wait upon the generosity of Sir Benjamin Guinness who paid for the restoration of the whole at a cost of £160,000 between 1860 and 1864. His sons continued the work until the end of the century, along with other work on redeveloping the neighbourhood, which swept away not only slums but also the ancient street market that was such a colourful feature of the area. Further restoration was carried out in 1972.

As a result of rebuilding and restoration, little remains of the medieval fabric except two pillars and the roofs of the choir vaults. Today the cathedral is one of the largest in Ireland, over 300 feet long and 56 feet high at the nave, its magnificence undiminished. The cathedral is filled with monuments, of which the most remarkable is the sixteenth-century Boyle memorial beside the Baptistry. In the north transept are many to the Royal Irish Regiment, on whom the first shots of the American Revolution were fired at Lexington Green in 1776.

The one great figure associated with the cathedral was Jonathan Swift, Dean from 1713 to 1745, whose memorial can be seen in the south aisle. Of interest too is the memorial to Carolan the harper, erected by the novelist Lady Morgan. Buildings associated with the cathedral are the Deanery, the Choir School and Marsh's Library.

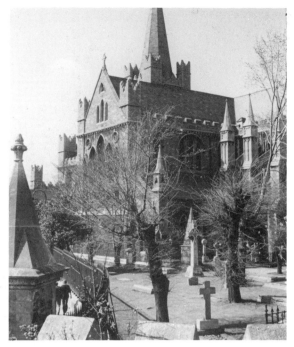

A view of the cathedral, looking across the cemetery from Marsh's Library.
PHOTO BORD FAILTE

St Patrick's from the old street market about 1890.
PAINTING BY WALTER OSBORNE. NATIONAL GALLERY OF IRELAND

The cathedral in winter from the north-east corner of St Patrick's Park.
PHOTO BORD FAILTE

The west front of St Patrick's in 1793.
PAINTING BY JAMES MALTON. NATIONAL GALLERY OF IRELAND

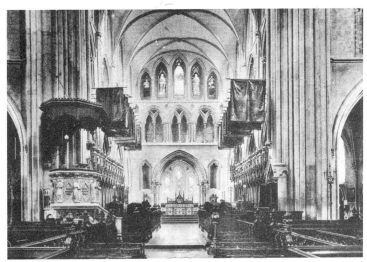

Choir of the cathedral hung with the banners of the Knights of St Patrick.
AUTHOR'S COLLECTION

Monuments in the north aisle.
LAWRENCE COLLECTION. NATIONAL LIBRARY OF
IRELAND

*Monument to Dean Swift in the south
aisle.*
AUTHOR'S COLLECTION

Interior of St Patrick's before restoration.
PAINTING BY JOHN CRUISE. NATIONAL GALLERY OF IRELAND

Christ Church Cathedral, Winetavern Street

[CHURCH OF IRELAND]

Lying within the old city walls, Christ Church was founded by Sitric, the Norse king of Dublin in 1038, for Dunan (Donough), first Bishop of Dublin. Legend claims that there was a church here even before Patrick and that he celebrated Mass there, prophesying a wonderful future for the church. A pleasant legend, which conceals the fact that there had been an old Celtic church on this site, the church of Cele Chriost, a foundation mentioned in the ninth century.

The first cathedral was a wooden one, along the lines of the stave churches which survive still in Norway. This was replaced in Norman times by a stone structure, erected in 1172 by St Laurence O'Toole, in the contemporary Norman style. The rest of the work was completed by John Comyn and Henry de Loundres between 1181 and 1225. Much of this transitional work between Norman and early gothic survived until the nineteenth century. It is dedicated to the Holy Trinity.

Over the centuries Christ Church has been extended and modified, but the fabric decayed after the Reformation. In 1652 the roof collapsed taking with it much of the fabric on the south and west sides. Huge buttresses were built and the windows filled up to strengthen the walls, leaving the south side an ugly mass of masonry by 1766. With the disestablishment of the Church of Ireland, a programme of serious restoration was undertaken between 1871 and 1878 by G.E. Street, which was entirely paid for by the Dublin distiller Henry Roe. What the visitor sees today is in fact mostly Street's handiwork. Street restored much of what he thought had been once in situ, but had also to add a great deal to the fabric.

The tomb of Strongbow, which is one of the sights of the church, is actually a memorial brought into the church at a later date, the real one having been vandalised. The tower dates only from 1600, and the Synod House, reached by a charming bridge, is from the nineteenth century (though it incorporates the tower of the medieval parish church of St Michael). This has now been sold by the Church of Ireland.

The vaults under the cathedral were once thought to date back to Norse times but are in fact medieval. Here can be seen the tabernacle used for the Catholic Mass when it was celebrated in the cathedral during the brief Dublin reign of James II in October 1689, before his defeat at the Boyne.

The west door of the cathedral opens into Winetavern Street, which runs down to the river. This was once a street of tall, crooked houses, many of them actually taverns. In the sixteenth century taverners had got to occupy the crypt of the church. A Dublin wit of the day commented:

Spirits above and spirits below,
Spirits divine and spirits - of wine.

The old cathedral, about 1820, with the buttressed west wall and old houses on Winetavern Street.
DRAWING BY PETER COSTELLO AFTER PETRIE

The newly restored cathedral, in a wood engraving of 1888.
AUTHOR'S COLLECTION

The rood screen erected by Street which was the subject of controversy.
LAWRENCE COLLECTION. NATIONAL LIBRARY OF IRELAND

The south side of the cathedral from Christ Church Place, with the bridge to the Synod House.
PHOTO BORD FAILTE

The crypt of the cathedral, often said to be Norse, actually medieval in date.
PHOTO BORD FAILTE

The north side of the cathedral from Winetavern Street.
PHOTO PETER COSTELLO

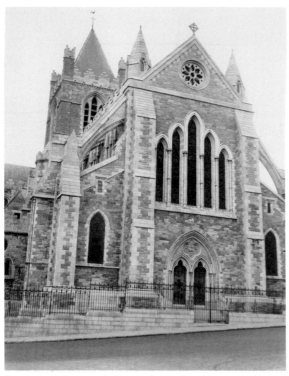

The west door of the cathedral, as restored.
PHOTO PETER COSTELLO

Lamb and Flag relief over west door.
PHOTO BORD FAILTE

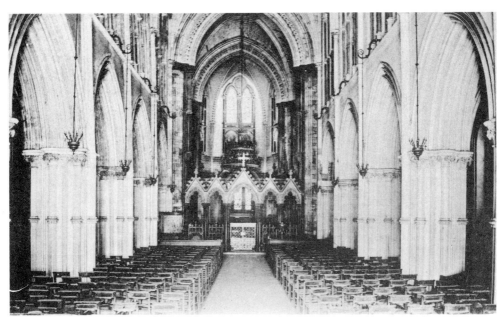

The nave of the cathedral, with the new rood screen erected by G.E. Street.
AUTHOR'S COLLECTION

St Mary's Pro-Cathedral, Marlborough Street

[ROMAN CATHOLIC]

After the Reformation when the city cathedrals continued in the hands of the Church of Ireland, the Roman Catholic Archbishops of Dublin used a chapel in Francis Street as their metropolitan church. In the eighteenth century this was transferred to St Mary's, a chapel in Liffey Street (now vanished). After the easing of the restrictions on Catholics, it was mooted that a new metropolitan church should be built on a site in Sackville Street, but this scheme came to nothing and the GPO stands there today.

Another site was acquired in Marlborough Street and there work was commenced in 1815. The severely classical design is thought to be by John Sweetman (though this is by no means certain), who based his concept on Grecian models as well as the church of St Philippe-le-Roule in Paris. The names of John Taylor and George Papworth are also associated with the completion of the work. The dome was added as an afterthought, and was objected to at the time. The high altar was by Turnerelli, and the relief of the Ascension by Smyth. The church was dedicated in 1825, and the old chapel closed.

The church is small, but has been the scene of many national events from the funeral of Daniel O'Connell to that of Michael Collins. The Palestrina Choir, in which John McCormack had his start, was founded by Edward Martyn during the heyday of the Irish Revival. More recently religious dramas have been presented in the church, very much in the manner of medieval times. In the 1880s it became customary to refer to this church as the 'Pro-Cathedral', to emphasise a long held nationalist feeling that one of the original medieval cathedrals should be 'returned' to Catholic hands.

When plans were drawn up after 1916 for a new Dublin, the notion was for a new cathedral on the north side of the city. In a revised plan of 1946 the cathedral was placed on the quays. But the archdiocese of Dublin preferred the idea of building on the south side, and the park in Merrion Square, facing the Dail, was bought as a site in the 1920s. As long as Dr McQuaid was alive this scheme never lapsed, but after his death a more realistic approach led Dr Ryan to give the park to the city in 1974. So Dublin in the eyes of many Catholics still lacks a truly dignified cathedral. But most suspect that the time is past when such a thing could be built. In St Mary's Dublin has in reality a fine building, more than worthy of the status of cathedral.

Exterior of the Pro-Cathedral, showing
the classical façade and the additional
dome.
LAWRENCE COLLECTION. NATIONAL LIBRARY OF
IRELAND

Interior of the church about 1899, with
the traditional arrangement of the
throne, altar, stalls and pulpit.
LAWRENCE COLLECTION. NATIONAL LIBRARY
OF IRELAND

*Detail from the base of the Cullen
memorial showing the Sisters of Charity
at work relieving the sick and needy of
Dublin.*
PHOTO PETER COSTELLO

*Memorial to Archbishop Murray in the
south aisle of the Pro-Cathedral.*
PHOTO PETER COSTELLO

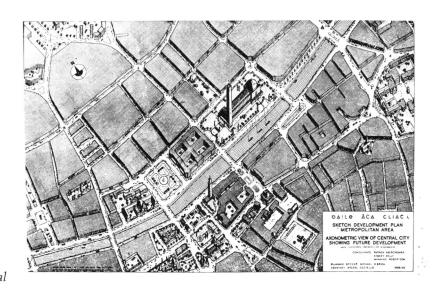

*Vision of a riverside Catholic cathedral
that never was, from Prof.
Abercrombie's 1940s plan for Dublin.*
AUTHOR'S COLLECTION

St Audoen's, Cornmarket

[CHURCH OF IRELAND]

Standing on the highest part of the old city of Dublin, St Audoen's is not only the most ancient site, but is the oldest fabric, still retaining much of its original Norman stone from 1190. The dedication is to a Norman saint, St Ouen; the original Celtic church here was dedicated to St Columcille.

What remains today is, of course, only part of the whole. Lord Portlester's Chapel (unroofed in 1773) is in state care, and contains the tomb of that noble, a Chancellor of Ireland. This part of St Audoen's is a ruin, but the rest of the fabric was restored in 1826 and at later dates. The tower, also restored at that time, was built in 1670 and hangs three bells made in 1423, which are said to be the oldest in Ireland.

At the Reformation the novelties of worship were not welcome at St Audoen's at first, where the priests resisted the changes sought by the first Anglican Archbishop of Dublin. The church had a long connection with the Mayor and Corporation of Dublin, only broken at the end of the last century. Originally St Audoen's was a prosperous church, patronised by rich merchants. But by late Georgian times a decline had set in; the Protestant population fell from 800 in 1831 to 274 in 1881.

In the porch of the church there can be seen, firmly clamped to the wall, the 'Lucky Stone' — an early Christian gravestone — to which many strange tales are attached. Dating from the eighth century, how it came to the church is not known, though there is a reference to it in 1309. It stood at the corner of the tower where it could be touched by passersby. In 1826 it was stolen and carried away, but was recovered after many misadventures. At the end of the last century it was fixed in the porch. Several tales connect a ghostly priest with it, and the stone itself is said to have occult virtues.

Sir Thomas Drew, writing in 1866, was the first architect to take a serious and detailed interest in the church. He and others ensured its survival. A fresco uncovered at this time of a Madonna and Child has since been weathered away.

Since 1974 St Audoen's has been part of the St Patrick's group of inner-city churches. The services are today held inside a small chapel, rather than in the whole church. The churchyard has now been turned into a park, winning a conservation award. Recent restoration work has exposed the interior stone-work, repointed the outside and reinforced the tower. The church bells, silent since 1898, have rung out again on Sundays with the help of ringers from the cathedrals and the Augustinian church nearby.

St Audoen's exterior today from the churchyard park.
DUBLIN CORPORATION

Interior of St Audoen's about 1890.
LAWRENCE COLLECTION. NATIONAL LIBRARY OF IRELAND

St Werburgh's, Werburgh Street

[CHURCH OF IRELAND]

St Werburgh's appears on Charles Brooking's 1728 map of Dublin in a more elaborate form than now exists: the top of the church was removed in 1810 as unsafe, though some say it was because it would have provided a revolutionary sniper with a point of vantage over the Castle Yard.

The grand classical façade, with its confident certainties, is all that remains of the original 1715 church by Burgh. The interior, more recently restored, is by John Smyth and dates from 1759. The stucco work in the chancel is by Michael Maguire. The gothic pulpit, which contrasts with the more austere style of the building, comes from the chapel in Dublin Castle.

In early times there had been a church dedicated to St Martin (the uncle of St Patrick, according to tradition) in this area. But the present church was founded in Norman times, and dedicated to St Werburgh, the patroness of Chester (then the sea-port for Dublin). The men of Chester used to use the church as a convivial meeting place. This church was once the most fashionable in Dublin, and was used by the Viceroy until the erection of the Chapel Royal. His private pew in the gallery under the organ is marked by a crown. Handel played here, and James Ussher the historian and later Archbishop of Armagh was an incumbent.

In the porch have been erected monuments from the vanished churches of St John's in Fishamble Street, and St Bride's in Bride Street. In the eighteenth century the city fire engine, little more than a large cart, was kept near the main entrance to the church, where it survives still.

The patriot Lord Edward Fitzgerald is buried in the Geraldine family burying place in the vaults. In the graveyard behind the church lies Henry Charles Sirr, the notorious Town-Major who arrested and fatally wounded him. Here also can be seen the curious gravestone of John Edwin, an actor in the Crow Street Theatre, who died of grief after a bad review:

Tis strange the mind, that very fiery particle,
Should let itself be snuffed out by an article.

The church as part of the modern street scene.
PHOTO PETER COSTELLO

Interior of St Werburgh's showing original galleries, the plain glass windows and the gothic pulpit brought in from the Chapel Royal, Dublin Castle.
AUTHOR'S COLLECTION

The front of St Werburgh's from Charles Brooking's map (1728).
AUTHOR'S COLLECTION

St Andrew's, St Andrew Street

[CHURCH OF IRELAND]

The medieval church of St Andrew was situated on the site of the old Norse pagan sanctuary near the City Hall. The dedication was moved after the Restoration to a church near the Thing Mount where the Norse held their assemblies.

The architect, William Dodson, produced an elliptical plan from which the odd church with its cone-shaped roof and crenellations came to be nicknamed 'The Round Church'.

This church, which was the special chapel of the Irish parliament, was demolished to make way for a new church in 1800; all that survives of it is a statue of the saint by Edward Smyth in the porch.

It was replaced by another round church designed by Francis Johnston, a concept which was strikingly modern in layout. This was fitted out in what was called 'Egyptian style' and the windows were covered with oil-silk transparencies rather than stained glass.

This church was destroyed by fire in 1860 and replaced by the present church, designed for a competition by W.H. Lynn, of Lanyon, Lynn and Lanyon, which was completed in 1862. His original conception called for rebuilding the whole neighbourhood in the same gothic style. The church is a fine piece of work, but situated so that it is very difficult to gain a clear view of it. From the surrounding streets the spire is the most obvious feature, the bulk of the building being obscured. The north aisle has been partitioned off to make a Chapel of Healing, in which the special healing mission of the Church of Ireland has been established since the 1950s. Here petitions are received, and special services conducted. This chapel contains many tablets commemorating the church's connection with families long in business in the neighbourhood, the Dublin Stock Exchange being located nearby.

The interior of the church is plain, the most interesting feature being in fact the head of St Andrew over the main door. There is a memorial to the dead of the Great War inside the church, but the unusual memorial in the churchyard is to Dublin soldiers killed in the Boer War.

The spire of St Andrew's from College Green.
PHOTO PETER COSTELLO

St Ann's, Dawson Street

[CHURCH OF IRELAND]

Here again a church appears on Brooking's map of 1728 in a form which was never finished, the elaborate façade designed by Isaac Wills in 1720 being reduced to a simpler form. The parish had been created in 1707, and when it was built the church was part of the expansion of the city into an area which was to become a major Georgian development up to the banks of the Grand Canal.

In 1868 the church was refronted with the present polychrome Romanesque façade by Sir Thomas Deane, though this too was left without the finishing touch of a planned-for tower. To Victorian times belong the stained glass windows, which for some detract from the Georgian purity of the interior with its elaborate wood and plaster-work. The Venetian mosaic reredos belongs, however, to the early part of this century. The church is remarkable for the very large number of memorial tablets, among which is one to Mrs Felicia Hemans, author of *Casabianca*, the poem with those immortal lines about the boy on the burning deck, who died in Dublin in 1835. In the north gallery is a memorial to Sir Hugh Lane, the nephew of Lady Gregory, to whom the city of Dublin owes many of the finest pictures in the Municipal Gallery.

Today St Ann's is very much an active city church, with various services, a social centre and bookshop. Older Dubliners still regret the passing of the Molesworth Hall and School at the rere of the church, for which delightful creations the modern church hall is a very inferior replacement. The church, however, is nearly always open, and even has people to pray in it. In 1723 Lord Newton left the sum of £13 a year for the distribution of bread to the poor, and the shelves installed to carry his munificence are still in use.   A few loaves are available after Sunday and early Monday services for deserving cases without distinction of religion.

St Ann's today
DRAWING BY PETER COSTELLO

*The front of St Ann's as planned in the
1720s from Brooking's map (1728).*

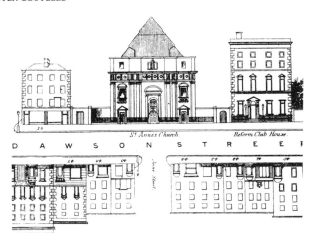

*St Ann's façade before it was refronted by Deane from
Shaw's Dublin Pictorial Guide (1850)*

St Andrew's, Westland Row

[ROMAN CATHOLIC]

Built in 1832-7 to the designs of John Boulger (or James Bolger, according to other authorities), to replace a smaller chapel situated in Townsend Street. The great Doric portico is surmounted by a statue of St Andrew bearing his cross. The church is cruciform in plan with a cupola over the intersection. The altar consists of four huge pillars of scagliolo, surmounted by a pediment. Inside this is a painting (now restored) by G.F. Beghley, *The Descent from the Cross* (1754). Among the other paintings and art works are *The Martyrdom of St Thomas à Becket* and *The Crucifixion* (both presented by Daniel O'Connell), *The Ascension* a sculpture by John Hogan, and a Madonna by William Pearse (Patrick's brother) in the mortuary chapel. The sanctuary ceiling is decorated with medallions of the Coronation of the Virgin, St Andrew and other saints.

Daniel O'Connell (who lived nearby in Merrion Square) was much involved with the erection of the church, which cost £13,000 and when finished was the largest in the city. The classical style was the preferred Catholic one in the early part of the nineteenth century, perhaps because it echoed the Baroque churches of Rome rather than the gothic bravura then favoured by the Anglicans.

Dubliners often referred to this church as 'All Hallows', the name of the original abbey from which Trinity College was erected. In *Ulysses*, Joyce brings Mr Bloom here belatedly to a Mass he watches with confused notions, pondering the mystery of the Eucharist.

Though built into a run of domestic houses the church and the attached presbytery and school are a lesson in integration. Though the altar has been changed to conform to the new liturgy, the church as a whole is unchanged, and the Victorian style remains largely intact. Among the many pious and sober memorials, the Farrell family tablet strikes an oddly pagan classical note.

St Andrew's church in Joyce's day.
LAWRENCE COLLECTION. NATIONAL LIBRARY IRELAND

Farrell family memorial.
PHOTO PETER COSTELLO

Original holy-water stoop in the church porch.
PHOTO PETER COSTELLO

St Michael and St John, Blind Quay

[ROMAN CATHOLIC]

On what had been the site of the famous Smock Alley Theatre, this parish church was built in 1815, to the designs of J. Taylor. A part of the theatre remains as a vaulted passage on the south-eastern side of the church, with what had been the pit of the theatre forming the vaults of the church. The renovated granite façade is simpler than the interior, which features elaborate gothic plaster pendants and pilasters, gothicised side chapels, organ gallery and confessionals.

The name of the church unites the title of the old medieval parish church of St John's (which was in Fishamble Street), and the penal chapel of St Michael in Rosemary Lane, which was in use up to 1815.

The church contains the remains of Fr Thomas Betagh, an eighteenth-century Jesuit who founded the classical school in Cook Street, a forerunner of the other more celebrated Jesuit schoools in the city today. His conspicuous monument (by Turnerelli) was paid for by the citizens of Dublin in appreciation of his educational achievements. On this church was hung the first bell to ring for Mass and the Angelus in Dublin since the Reformation. As this was a technical illegality, threats of prosecution were made against the parish priest, Fr Michael Blake, by Alderman Carlton, an evangelical Protestant and Orangeman, but when the aid of Daniel O'Connell was called upon, the parish priest was troubled no more.

For some time closure and even demolition hung over this church in recent years. Plans were under way to turn it into a museum, when the opportunity to utilise it again for the officially sanctioned celebration of Mass in the Tridentine Rite gave it a new lease of life in 1989. A proposal for developing the neighbouring quay (involving the demolition of the old parish schools) will make the church the centrepiece of an imaginative scheme of urban renewal.

SS Michael and John from the Liffey quays.
PHOTO PETER COSTELLO

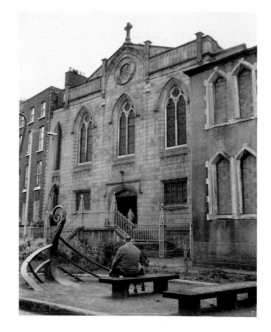

The church exterior has now been enhanced by a millennium sculpture of a Norse boat.
PHOTO PETER COSTELLO

The Immaculate Conception (Adam and Eve's), Merchant's Quay

[FRANCISCAN FATHERS]

Evoked by James Joyce in the opening passage of *Finnegans Wake*, Adam and Eve's with its great green copper dome is a major landmark in the skyscape of Dublin and in the imagination of its citizens. The great church which we see today was founded in 1834 on the spot where the penal chapel of St Michael had stood once. Before the time of the Reformation the Franciscan Fathers had been established in Dublin in a friary on the site of what is now St Nicholas of Myra. When they were driven from there by penal regulations, they established themselves in secrecy in a small room behind a tavern in Cook Street called 'Adam and Eve's', through which people would enter to hear Mass. Hence the popular name for the present church.

This church, designed by Patrick Byrne, has been enlarged and expanded and now opens out on to Merchant's Quay. It has been worked over in 1923 and 1959, so that the present structure is largely new, the style being a classically inspired Romanesque.

St Teresa's Church, Clarendon Street

[DISCALCED CARMELITE FATHERS]

Here is a late eighteenth-century church which had to be built, as required by law, off the main highway and with little outward show of being a church. The monastery was built above the church so the original appearance was much like a private house. The foundation stone was laid in 1793 by John Sweetman, the Dublin brewer, who bought the site in his own name for the Carmelites. Robert Emmet and the poet Thomas Moore were among those who subscribed to the building fund. The rebellion of 1798 disrupted the work, with workers being arrested. The church was opened to the public in 1810, being the first Dublin church authorised by parliament after the passing of the Catholic Relief Bill of 1793.

However, the simple original church has been much enlarged since then, until St Teresa's is among the most distinguished of Dublin's churches. The sanctuary, eastern transept and the campanile were built in 1863. The western transept, and the façade surmounted by statues of the Virgin, St Teresa and St John of the Cross facing on to Clarendon Street, were erected in 1876. The rose window which is the main feature of this extension depicts various Carmelite saints.

Adam and Eve's: the exterior view from Cook Street.
The far side of the church faces on to Merchant's Quay.
PHOTO PETER COSTELLO

A High Mass being celebrated about 1932
in Adam and Eve's.
PHOTO COURTESY FRANCISCAN LIBRARY

Façade of St Teresa's in Clarendon Street.
PHOTO PETER COSTELLO

Our Lady of Mount Carmel, Whitefriars Street

[CALCED CARMELITE FATHERS]

The Carmelite Friars had been prominent among the Orders of medieval Dublin with an abbey in this area, hence the name Whitefriars Street. Expelled at the time of the Reformation, they eventually returned, and after moving about the city the opportunity arose in the early nineteenth century to buy a site on the street still named for their order.

Designed by George Papworth, the church was opened in 1827. At that time it faced about in the opposite direction. It has since been realigned and extended, and a new entrance built through the monastery into Aungier Street, so that the present building is largely recent work.

The shrines in this church are among the most popular in the city, especially those of St Ann, to whom there was always a strong local devotion, and St Valentine the Martyr, whose remains were presented to the monastery by the Pope.

But the most interesting object in the church is the fifteenth-century carved wooden statue of the Virgin, Our Lady of Dublin. This is thought to have come originally from St Mary's Abbey, and to be the very statue from which the golden crown was removed to crown Lambert Simnel as King Edward VI in 1487. After the dissolution of the abbey, the statue was neglected, then lost. It was eventually recovered by the prior of Whitefriars Street, Fr Pratt, from a local antique shop. He learned that it had been turned upside down and used as a trough and that this odd fate had preserved it. Stylistically it seems to be German in origin, though it is not from the hand of Dürer, as is often claimed. From any point of view it is one of the most remarkable objects in Dublin.

Interior of Whitefriars church as it was originally.
ENGRAVING AFTER GEORGE PETRIE

Modernised interior.
PHOTO PETER COSTELLO

Late medieval statue of the Virgin (Our Lady of Dublin), engraved soon after it was rediscovered by Fr Pratt.
PHOTO PETER COSTELLO

St Catherine of Alexandria, Meath Street

[ROMAN CATHOLIC]

Though the date of its actual constitution is unknown, St Catherine's is one of the oldest of the parishes outside the old city walls. St Catherine was an Alexandrian martyr of the fourth century, who was executed bound to a spiked wheel, with which she is always depicted, hence the name of the familiar firework.

The original penal parish church was at Bridgefoot Street (then called Dirty Lane), off Thomas Street, leading down to the Liffey. However, in 1782 it was removed to the present site in Meath Street, in what was a more salubrious area of the district.

That Georgian church was replaced by the present Victorian church, designed by J.J. McCarthy, which was begun in 1852 and opened six years later in 1858. The plans were very elaborate, for a nave with open timbered roof, side aisles and chapel at an estimated cost of up to £9,000. In fact it was built for £6,000. As is so common in Dublin, the intended tower was never completed, the stub being finished off later with a machiolated parapet.

The interior is finely done, though plain. The painting (now much darkened) in the architrave of the sanctuary, *The Martyrdom of St Catherine*, is by Dubliner William MacBride. The most impressive feature of the church is the great east window which floods the sanctuary with light, matched by an equally impressive west window, which has (unusually for McCarthy) perpendicular panelled tracery. But the church is not the equal of its neighbours in John's Lane or Francis Street, being simpler in conception and finish.

St Catherine's still serves a vigorous inner-city community in the neighbourhood of Thomas Street. In the heart of the Liberties of Dublin, this area represents the 'real Dublin' beloved of many, a neighbourhood of both rich humanity and terrible poverty. The Corporation of Dublin has not been the best friend of the citizens here, for though there has been a certain amount of urban renewal, whole streets have been allowed to tumble into ruins.

The writer Eamonn Mac Thomais has drawn on the traditions of these streets in a series of evocative, if sentimental books, which have proved very popular with many who would never visit these streets themselves. On weekdays when the market stalls are active, Meath Street is certainly a lively and noisy place.

Exterior of St Catherine's today.
PHOTO PETER COSTELLO

A baptismal ceremony welcomes a new member of the community.
PHOTO PETER COSTELLO

St Catherine's about 1900.
LAWRENCE COLLECTION. NATIONAL LIBRARY OF IRELAND

St Nicholas of Myra, Francis Street

[ROMAN CATHOLIC]

In medieval times the site of this church was a Franciscan monastery, which was destroyed at the time of the Reformation. In the seventeenth century, however, the Franciscans had actually reacquired the land for their own use, when the difficulties following on the Titus Oates plot in 1678 made them reconsider their plans. The site was then used for a parish church to replace a chapel in Limerick Lane, which connected Francis Street and Patrick Street. The first parish priest was appointed in 1709. The church was a very fine and well-appointed one, and for a long time served the Catholic Archbishops of Dublin as their metropolitan church.

The present church, designed by John Leeson, was begun in 1829, opened in 1834 and finally dedicated in 1854. It was classical in conception, but the Ionic portico, pediment, bell-tower and cupola, which are the main exterior features of the church today, are the work of Patrick Byrne in 1860. The figures on the pediment are of Our Lady, St Patrick, and St Nicholas of Myra (the original Santa Claus), distinguished by the three golden balls symbolic of charity still used by money lenders. The anchor, which lies at his feet, was also a symbol of hope.

Inside the church, the Pietà and the two angels above and beside the main altar are the work of John Hogan, who was also responsible for the gesso-work relief of the Last Supper and the Marriage of the Virgin (based on Perugine's painting). The altar itself was imported from Italy.

Above the sanctuary the ceiling is decorated with paintings of the Twelve Apostles, each with his appropriate symbol, in the central circle; and on the four corners of the crossing, four Fathers of the Church: Gregory, Ambrose, Jerome and Augustine. In the entablature of the pediment above the altar appears the very ancient symbol of the all-seeing eye of God.

Among the stained glass windows, there is one by Harry Clarke of the Marriage of Our Lady and St Joseph, in the Nuptial Chapel, where it has witnessed thousands of Dublin marriages. Other windows include St Patrick, St Nicholas of Myra, cradling in his arm a model of the church, and St Thomas à Becket (after whom Thomas Street is named).

In the middle of old Dublin, St Nicholas, a fine late Georgian church, represents a connected tradition going back to 1192, when John Comyn reserved a chapel in St Patrick's as the parish church of St Nicholas-without-the-Walls; while St Nicholas-Within dates from 1166.

St Nicholas of Myra today. The three statues are twentieth-century additions grafted on to the classical façade.
PHOTO PETER COSTELLO

The front of St Nicholas, viewed from the slums of Wall's Lane, about 1910.
LAWRENCE COLLECTION. NATIONAL LIBRARY OF IRELAND

St James's, James Street
[ROMAN CATHOLIC]

The expansion of Dublin brought about the separation of St James's from St Catherine's parish in 1724. A small chapel, built about 1754, was outgrown in less than a century; the site of this has now been absorbed into the Guinness Brewery complex.

The foundation stone of a new church was laid in 1844 by Daniel O'Connell. The gothic design by Patrick Byrne was completed and opened in 1854, when the old chapel was closed and the site sold off. The interesting exterior, with its peaks and pinnacles and square tower over the main entrance, is more interesting than the interior, which has not worn well. Though there is a vigorous parish life, lack of money (which the clergy prefer to spend on people rather than buildings) means that there is always a shortage. As result the interior has become shabby and run down. However, with the various parish houses, and the tree-planted open space to the south, the church blooms in the midst of a largely industrial scene.

The parish was an old one, which is connected by tradition with the medieval pilgrimage to the shrine of St James at Compostela in northern Spain. This was one of the major pilgrimages of Christendom, and one of the most popular in medieval Ireland. About here in the centuries after the Reformation was the edge of the city, where many Catholics lived.

The most important factor for the whole district in recent centuries has been the rise to pre-eminence of Guinness's out of the numerous brewers of eighteenth-century Dublin. This was a firm on which much of working-class Dublin depended in the days when there was little more than casual labour in the city for the majority of men. The museum in the brewery gives a vivid impression to the visitor of the life of the area in the last century or so.

The Grand Canal, by which much of the country's trade was carried in the days before trains, ran into a harbour behind this church which has now been filled in, leaving only its memory in the titles of some public houses and the name of Basin Street. But much of the land to the back of the church has fallen into unrelieved urban squalor, appalling to the tourist, frightening to the Dubliner.

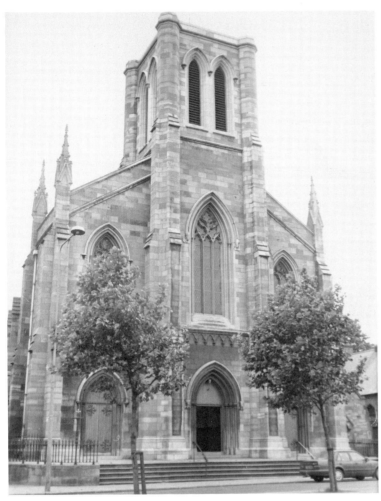

Front façade of the church.
PHOTO PETER COSTELLO

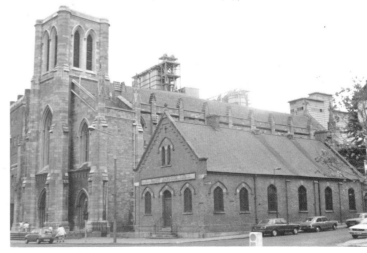

St James's church, with parish school and the
encroaching brewery to the rere.
PHOTO PETER COSTELLO

St Augustine and St John, Thomas Street

[AUGUSTINIAN FRIARS]

The present building dates from 1862, but it was erected on the part of the ancient abbey of St John, hence St John's Lane, the popular name of the church among Dubliners.

It was in the surviving tower of the abbey that the Augustinians established themselves when they left the Bakers' Hall at St Audoen's Court in 1704. A chapel was established there and by 1731 there were eight priests in the community. After 1745, when the Jacobite threat was lifted, conditions for the Orders improved greatly. In 1781 the friars enlarged the chapel into a church and built a house. Dr Matthew Carr, a prior of the period, was denounced in 1798 as 'a democrat', which won him the praise of George Washington.

In 1860 it was decided to erect a more substantial church. The architect selected was Edward Welby Pugin (son of the famous Pugin) who was working then with George Ashlin. It is said that Ruskin looking over the architect's shoulder murmured that the church would be 'a poem in stone' — a fable for which architectural historians have been unable to uncover a good authority. The style of French decorated gothic was very much in the great tradition of Pugin's father.

The foundation stone of what was to be one of the city's most elaborate churches was laid at Easter 1862, but the work took some thirty-three years to complete. The foreman and many of the workmen were Fenians who were in trouble with the government authorities in 1865. For this reason St John's Lane was nicknamed 'the Fenian church'.

The spire and roof were completed in 1874 when the nave was opened for public Masses. Work resumed in 1892, and the exterior was completed by 1895, the interior by 1911, under the supervision of Ashlin and Coleman. Coleman was justly proud of the achievement, writing that 'the front is, perhaps the noblest and most striking façade of ecclesiastical art in this country.'

The red sandstone which was used for the intricate gothic dressings has weathered badly, and has had to undergo extensive repair work in recent years. The tower, a prominent city landmark, rises 50 feet. It was designed by William Hague. The statues of the Apostles are by James Pearse, the father of the Pearse brothers.

The interior of church would still delight Ruskin, for it retains all the fine mid-Victorian work. The chapel of Our Lady of Good Counsel (1898), with its wrought iron-work, is especially fine. A member of the community, Professor F.X. Martin, was the leading figure in the thwarted efforts to save the Viking remains on nearby Wood Quay from being built over by new city offices. Now a campaign to preserve St John's Lane itself is underway.

Front of St Augustine and St John, Ruskin's 'poem in stone'.
PHOTO BORD FAILTE

Chapel of Our Lady of Good Counsel with its cast and wrought ironwork.
PHOTO KEN MACGOWAN/IRISH PRESS

St Audoen's, High Street

[ROMAN CATHOLIC]

In an area rich in churches, St Audoen's is now less used as a parish church and is devoted more to other educational and religious activities, including a video presentation of the Ireland of St Patrick.

The post-Reformation chapel was in Cook Street, behind St Audoen's arch, though when the Dominicans removed to the north side of the river, the parish took over their chapel at Bridge Street, a lost church dating from 1719 which was closed in 1846. The present church, built between 1841 and 1847 to the designs of Patrick Byrne, stands on a site hard by the more ancient Anglican church of the same dedication. Indeed, the east end of Lord Portlester's chapel is attached to the side wall of the church.

The dome, which was a main feature of the original fabric, collapsed in 1880 and was not rebuilt. The portico, with its Grecian pillars, was erected in 1898 and is the work of Stephen Ashlin and Patrick Byrne. The piazza to the front of the church was laid out also at this date, along with the enclosing railings. These additions make an attractive finish to what is a rather grim building with black limestone walls of forbidding aspect when viewed from Cook Street.

The interior retains much of its early elegance, with fluted Corinthian pilasters, cornices and high-level windows, and a coffered ceiling with barrel vaulting. Professor Abercrombie, the architect who devoted much energy to replanning Dublin, considered St Audoen's the finest church in Dublin. The high altar was a particular feature of the church, and the statue of Our Lady (1849) by Peter Bonanni (which was exhibited at the Dublin Exhibition of 1853) was much admired when it was installed on its side altar. (Sometimes attributed to Benzoni, this fine piece is a reminder of the days before Hogan came to the fore when no Irish artist could be expected to work on a church, and art works were imported wholesale from Italy.)

The local late medieval devotion to St Anne, whose feast day was enjoined universally on Catholics only in 1584 as a model for married women and child-carers, finds expression in a much patronised shrine, with a Deghini-cast statue of the saint.

The nave of the church has been arranged for video shows, with a screen which unrolls to close the transept crossing. A hooded monk brooding over his desk belongs to the new theatrical aspect of the church's life.

The holy-water stoops that flank the main entrance are unusual giant clam shells, which were installed in 1917. They were brought back from the Pacific by a sea captain who gave them as a gift to his brother, the parish priest of the day.

The front façade of St Audoen's about 1910.
LAWRENCE COLLECTION. NATIONAL LIBRARY OF IRELAND

One of the giant clam shells used as holy-water stoops.
PHOTO PETER COSTELLO

St Stephen's, Mount Street Crescent

[CHURCH OF IRELAND]

Called by all Dubliners 'The Pepper Canister', St Stephen's is the best-placed church in the whole of Dublin, for there are few views to equal the sight from Merrion Square of this church with its copper dome lit by the setting summer sun, framed between the Georgian houses of Mount Street. It backs on to the Grand Canal, that ultimate boundary of Georgian Dublin, with a less finished appearance of plain rubble masonry in contrast to the classical elegance of the portico.

The church was erected from the designs of John Bowden in 1824 and completed by John Welland in 1827, as a chapel-of-ease for St Peter's on the other side of St Stephen's Green. It was the last classical erection of the Established Church, and the details of the design were inspired by Erectheum, the Towers of the Winds and the Monument of Lysicrates — classical references which would have delighted contemporary worshippers.

This was the church of the most prosperous part of Dublin during a period of over 150 years, for Merrion Square was one of the main residences of the leading professional men of the Victorian era.

There were some 3,000 Protestant parishioners at the time of the Great War. By the 1960s this had declined to 300. A further reduction, however, has not prevented the church (now united with St Ann's) from remaining an active one, with musical seasons as well as regular services.

The church has given its name to the small private press for publishing his own poetry established by Thomas Kinsella, who lives nearby in Percy Place. Flann O'Brien (Brian O'Nolan) passed part of his childhood in a house in Herbert Place facing the canal. In Upper Mount Street which runs down to the church can be found the headquarters of two of the great political parties of modern Ireland. Though the immediate area of the church has been invaded by the inevitable modern office blocks, it remains among the few areas of the city where the true atmosphere of Georgian Dublin can still be savoured (though the church can only be seen at the time of Sunday services). An unusual addition to the streetscape is a bronze statue of a small girl swinging from a lamppost outside one of the office entrances, a gift to the city for Dublin's Millennium Year of 1988.

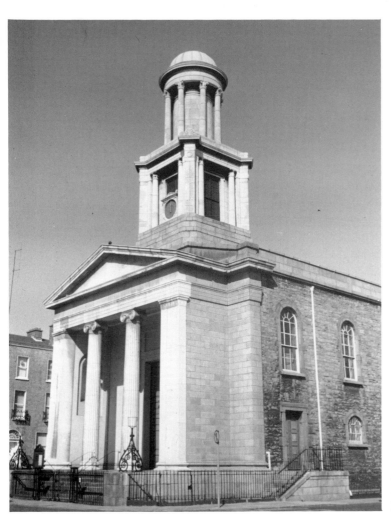

St Stephen's from Herbert Street, showing cut stone front and carp side walls.
PHOTO PETER COSTELLO.

St Stephen's façade from Upper Mount Street.
PHOTO PETER COSTELLO

Unitarian Church, St Stephen's Green

[UNITARIAN CHURCH]

Built in 1863 the gothic Unitarian church was designed by William H. Lynn of the firm of Lanyon, Lynn and Lanyon based in Belfast, after open competition. The church hall is reached by a ground-level door, while the school (now the Damer Hall, much used for plays) was to the rere. While the front façade is almost hectic in its varied planes, the rere aspect, almost lost in a canon of modern offices, is much simpler.

Though the roots of the theologically liberal Unitarian position are complex, going down into the earliest days of the Reformation and the swirling transformations of Dissent during the seventeenth and eighteenth centuries, the church itself was only legally organised in 1813, after the repeal of the relevant penal laws. In Northern Ireland many of the old Presbyterian churches became Unitarian.

This Dublin congregation traces itself back to the first group of Dissenters that arose in the city under Elizabeth I. Records exist of a meeting house in Wood Street which was opened in 1673, later moving to Strand Street in 1764. With the emergence of a fixed Unitarian point of view this congregration adopted its credal position, calling itself, as the communion plate in use here today reveals, 'The Unitarian Congregation Strand Street'.

The basic Unitarian belief is in an undivided Godhead, with Christ as a prophet rather than a divine being. Long associated with Lancashire and Boston, Unitarianism was a religion of Victorian business, a sensible unfussy no-nonsense creed perhaps. As a religious position Unitarianism is more ethical than enthusiastic, sharing little of the intolerance often found with more extreme Presbyterians.

Though they came from the chapel tradition, by the mid-nineteenth century the Unitarians were ready to adopt a more decorated style of architecture. For its period this is a model church. Its most interesting feature is its stained glass, much of it of English or Continental origin. Over the communion table, however, is one of the first pieces of glass to be made by the revived Irish industry. For half a century until 1962 the minister here was the well-known Rev. E. Savell Hicks.

The Unitarian Church, St Stephen's Green.
PHOTO PETER COSTELLO

University Church, St Stephen's Green

[ROMAN CATHOLIC]

W hen John Henry Newman answered the call of the Irish Hierarchy to come to Ireland to establish a university he entered upon an unhappy and unfruitful period of his life. It has left some permanent memorials, however: his lectures on the idea of a university, and this church in the heart of Dublin.

As part of his college plan he insisted upon a college chapel, for he thought it would provide a focus for the life of the staff and students. It was built in 1856 with the help of John Hungerford Pollen, like Newman a convert to Catholicism, whom he had invited to Dublin as Professor of Fine Art.

Newman had decided views against gothic as not being quite Christian enough, with its echoes of the pagan forests of Northern Europe. The only suitable style for a church was Byzantine, hence this splendid Romanesque masterpiece. It shows the influence of Ruskin's *Stones of Venice*, which came out in 1852.

Standing on a site to the rere of the range of Georgian houses and mansions along St Stephen's Green, it is reached through a decorated porch, and a rather bleak passage in which there is a memorial to the great Celticist Eugene O'Curry, the first Professor of Archaeology in the world.

Modelled on a Roman church, the marbles which decorate the walls are said to have been presented to Newman by the Pope. Above these (now much darkened from the action of the still-wet plaster when they were put up) are copies of Raphael's cartoons, which can be seen well only in the early morning light. A special feature is the gallery on the north wall, with its latticed windows, which in the East would have been reserved for women, but was here intended for the choir.

The sanctuary and altar, which are treated in full style with Our Lady as the Seat of Wisdom gloriously filling the roof of the apse, are among the finest things in any Dublin church, the work of Pollen himself. Before coming to Dublin Pollen had decorated the ceilings of an Oxford church and of Merton College. The ceiling here is finely decorated with a foliate design between the open beams.

The Lady Chapel was built as a gift from Mr Justice O'Brien. In the church are memorial busts of Newman himself (by Farrell, 1892), and of Thomas Arnold, the poet's brother, Professor of English in the college.

For a long time University Church was a chapel-of-ease to Harrington Street. It was much used both by university students and by university families until UCD moved to Belfield. It was made a full parish in 1974. It is a church held in great affection by those who used it in the old days, and it still sees many university weddings.

Interior of the church.
PHOTO COURTESY UNIVERSITY CHURCH

Presbyterian Church, Adelaide Road

[PRESBYTERIAN CHURCH IN IRELAND]

Built in 1840 as part of a ribbon development along the Grand Canal, this church stands at the head of Earlsfort Terrace, closing the vista from the National Concert Hall in a striking manner.

The classical style of the portico, with its main entrance reached by a flight of steps, contrasts with the gothic churches of the Church of Ireland and the Roman Catholics in the neighbourhood. The surrounding houses are very mixed, ranging in date from the 1830s to about 1900. This was a prosperous area in late Victorian times, well suited to Presbyterian businessmen and their families. The church itself is painted a dour colour which shows it up badly in its tree-shaded position.

The Presbyterians received a Toleration Act in 1719, and were supported by a state grant called the Regium Donum. Nevertheless like the Catholics and other Dissenters they fared badly during the course of the eighteenth century, many in fact emigrating to America. Their dissatisfaction brought many out in 1798 with the United Irishmen. But after the Union Presbyterians threw in their lot with the Unionist cause against the rise of Irish nationalism, and formed the backbone of the vigorous Orange resistance from the 1880s on to Home Rule.

In Dublin the earliest Presbyterian chapel that survives can still be seen in Eustace Street, a few doors from the Quakers, which seems to have been established before 1728 by English emigrants who followed an old-fashioned pattern. For many years this was used as a printers', but is now empty. However, the building with its segment-headed doors and windows with bolection mouldings is a fine one.

This church in Adelaide Road is a continuation of the same tradition, which after a century was moving out into the suburbs of the growing city. But the further passage of time has found Presbyterians in the south increasingly out of tune with their co-religionists in Ulster, their firmly held views well tempered by the experience of living in a largely Catholic, but usually tolerant, society.

For many years the archaeologist Professor R.A.S. Macalister played the organ in this church. The Donore Road congregation (who used a church on the South Circular Road, an account of which is given below under the Dublin Mosque) has now been united with this congregation.

The church hall is now used as an unemployment counselling centre, giving the church a practical weekday role in the local community.

Exterior of Adelaide Road Presbyterian Church.
PHOTO PETER COSTELLO

Detail of classical treatment.
PHOTO PETER COSTELLO

St Kevin's, Harrington Street
[ROMAN CATHOLIC]

The parish of St Kevin was created from St Catherine's in 1855. There had been an ancient Celtic church dedicated to St Kevin, the remains of which can be seen in a small park off Camden Row, which gave its name to the new church. The dedication suggests a Celtic foundation, though the first record dates only from 1226. This was long in use as an Anglican chapel (being unroofed only in 1922), and a place of pilgrimage for Catholics seeking the burial place of the martyr Archbishop Hurley (executed in 1584). The celebrated Jesuit of the eighteenth century, Fr John Austin, is buried there as well. The Anglican church of St Kevin (now deconsecrated) is in Bloomfield Avenue.

The Catholic church of St Kevin was designed by George Ashlin, an architect much favoured by the Catholic Church from his association with Pugin. (He also worked on Inchicore, Rathfarnham, and Tallaght, as well as on a portion of the renewals of St Peter's, Phibsborough.)

Work began in 1867, when the parish was created, and the church was completed in 1872, replacing a wooden church which had served as a chapel-of-ease to St Nicholas of Myra. The church was dedicated by Cardinal Cullen on the Feast of St Kevin, 3 June 1872.

The gothic style was typical of Pugin and Ashlin, and the symmetrical design of the architecture was much admired. The stained glass, which is inset in very large windows, was all of Irish workmanship. The size of the gothic windows are such that the church is flooded with light, giving it an airy and pleasant atmosphere. The gothic detail of the reredos and the pulpit is very fine. The cast iron ends to the pews in the front of the church are unusual.

Standing on a main artery of the city, the church was for a long time in one of the main areas of middle-class Dublin. Social changes since the 1930s have meant that the parish is now reduced in numbers, but St Kevin's, with its presbytery in Heytesbury Street and associated Christian Brothers' school in Synge Street, both in the same rustic granite masonry, remains one of the finest mid-Victorian churches in the city. George Bernard Shaw was born in Synge Street in 1856, and the painter Harry Kernoff had his studio in Stamer Street opposite from the 1940s until his death.

St Kevin's, Harrington Street.
PHOTO PETER COSTELLO

Pulpit and pews in St Kevin's.
PHOTO PETER COSTELLO

Grave of Fr John Austin S.J. with the old
St Kevin's church in the background.
PHOTO PETER COSTELLO

St Finian's, Adelaide Road

[LUTHERAN CHURCH IN IRELAND]

This small gothic edifice began life as a chapel of the Catholic Apostolic Church, the official name of the Irvingites. It was designed by E.T. Owen in 1863.

The Irvingites were among the more curious religious sects of the nineteenth century. Edward Irving (1792-1834) was a Scottish preacher and originally a member of the Church of Scotland. He came to London in 1822, and his sermons at a chapel in Hatton Garden soon drew notice. His book *For the Oracles of God* created a sensation. His thinking became increasingly divorced from Presbyterianism and he was eventually expelled. With the support of the banker Henry Drummond and others of the same class he formed the Catholic Apostolic Church. This was ruled by a set of twelve apostles, who alone could create priests. Under them were prophets (who could speak in tongues), evangelists, and angels or pastors. The distinctive creed of the church was a belief in the imminent return of the Lord and a pentecostal enthusiasm, of which speaking in tongues was only a part. The church drew widely on early Christian sources for a ritualistic service with an elaborate liturgy.

At its peak the sect numbered over 50,000. The Scottish writer Gavin Maxwell, in his memoirs *The House of Elrig*, gives a vivid account of his upbringing in the Catholic Apostolic Church, and of the life led by its adherents at Albury in Surrey. Alas the Lord did not come, the apostles died out, and today the church is without pastors, and upheld by a dwindling number of adherents. It was for the Irvingites that Christ Church, Gordon Square, London, one of the masterpieces of Victorian architecture, was created.

This Dublin church is a very tame example of the usual Irvingite style. With the decline of the Catholic Aspostolic Church it was passed to the Church of Ireland in 1933. For some years it was used to hold Anglican services in Gaelic, but this did not prove a popular cause in the city.

Eventually it was leased at a peppercorn rent to the Lutheran Church in Ireland, who hold services there in their native language for the German community in Ireland.

The wood-panelled interior is very plain and painted white. There are no relics of the Irvingites, the last of whom only recently passed from the Dublin scene, having been reduced to praying in an upper room in Westland Row.

St Finian's, formerly the Catholic Apostolic Church, Dublin.
PHOTO PETER COSTELLO

Jewish Synagogue, Adelaide Road

[DUBLIN HEBREW CONGREGATION]

There have been Jews in Ireland for some 500 years. The first communities were Sephardic Jews from Spain and Portugal who came here after their expulsion in 1492, many settling in ports along the southern coast.

However, the majority of Irish Jews arrived in Ireland as a consequence of the pogroms in Eastern Europe after 1880, most settling along the South Circular Road. This wave of emigration lasted until a few years before the Great War.

The site in Adelaide Road was bought in 1890, and the synagogue was built by 1892, when the older one in St Mary's Abbey closed. This was the first expressly built synagogue for Jewish worship in Ireland, and was designed in an appropriately oriental Byzantine style by J.J. O'Callaghan, at a cost of over £5,000. It sat about 450 people. There was an annexe for classrooms, the nucleus of a later national school. The building was extended to the rere in 1925 in the same fine brick-work.

Terenure Synagogue, Rathfarnham Road, Terenure

[TERENURE HEBREW CONGREGATION]

The synagogue of the Dublin Terenure Congregation was built in 1952. This is a modern-style building, designed by Wilfrid Cantwell, very typical of its period, which slopes to the rere from a modernist façade with five Star of David windows above an entrance porch. A simple enough building, it has been arranged in traditional orthodox style. The entrance porch contains a memorial window to the victims of Nazi persecution, and in the grounds is a memorial stone to fellow-Jews who were killed in the Holocaust.

The contrast between these buildings is a reminder that the backward look of the Jewish tradition is often allied with progressive social ideas. Here, too, the history of Europe in our time finds a meaningful Irish echo.

The Jewish population in Ireland has declined from a peak in about 1890, but those who have remained, less than 2,000, have made their mark on Irish society, playing leading roles in the worlds of politics, medicine, science and the arts.

Dublin Hebrew Congregation, Adelaide Road.
PHOTO PETER COSTELLO

Memorial at Terenure to the
Jewish victims of the Holocaust.
PHOTO PETER COSTELLO

Terenure Synagogue.
PHOTO PETER COSTELLO

Dublin Mosque, South Circular Road

[ISLAMIC COMMUNITY IN IRELAND]

This building was once the Donore Presbyterian Church, a small congregation living in this area of Dublin largely developed after 1880. At one time this was seen as the Jewish quarter of the city, with several synagogues. Today the flavour is quite different.

Arab culture had been represented in Dublin by the wonderful collections in the Chester Beatty Library, but Islam itself was alien to the city. The arrival of Muslim students from Libya, the Gulf States, and other countries began in the 1970s. The growth of Islamic business interests, from international meat companies to small corner shops selling chick peas and Halal meat, has led to the creation of an Islamic community along the South Circular Road, moving in among the last of the Jewish community there. At the five occasions of daily prayer the streets of the neighbourhood are full of men and their sons coming and going from the Mosque. According to the Imam of Dublin there are about 2,000 Muslims in the city. Plans for a Muslim national school have been agreed with the education authorities and only need a suitable site to go ahead.

Externally the building has not been changed except for the replacement of the Cross by a Crescent on the front gable peak. Internally the church has had all its pews removed to make way for a green-carpeted floor on which devout Muslims kneel and prostrate themselves five times a day in the direction of Mecca while imploring the blessings of Allah.

A gallery has been added on the west side of the building, while on the east a Mihrab (or prayer niche) and the raised pulpit for the Imam forms the only fixed feature of the room.

Beside the Mosque is an Islamic Centre with various services for the community, and a library with books both in Arabic and English on Islam which is open to visitors.

The Islamic community keep themselves very much to themselves, for their imaginations are focused completely on their own kind and on the events in the countries they come from. Yet the advent of Arab culture to Ireland has aroused in some Irish intellectuals an increasing interest not only in the Arab cultures generally but also in the Eastern origins of aspects of Irish culture. Early Christianity in Ireland was imported not from Europe but from Egypt, with its emphasis on desert hermitages, special privations and artistic conventions. It may be that ultimately the Islamic community will have a special, though now unforeseen, impact on Irish culture today.

The Dublin Mosque, South Circular Road.
PHOTO PETER COSTELLO

Interior of the mosque showing the pulpit and the prayer niche facing towards Mecca.
PHOTO PETER COSTELLO

Immaculate Heart of Mary, City Quay

[ROMAN CATHOLIC]

This church for the port of Dublin, facing Gandon's Custom House across the Liffey, was finished in 1863. The gates, railings and bell-tower were added during 1887-1900. The area was made a separate parish in 1908.

The original Catholic church for this neighbourhood had been St Andrew's chapel, first in Hawkins Street, later in Townsend Street, in which many dockers and sailors worshipped and were married until it closed in 1834. The new St Andrew's in Westland Row was further away from the docks towards a better district of the city. So this chapel-of-ease was opened in 1863. A writer in the 1920s described it as 'this pretty little edifice of Gothic design, handsomely embellished within, making an inviting retreat from the bustle and clangour of the quayside.' But this was to disguise the social reality.

Dublin towards the end of the century was a growing port, and it was the increase in population which led to the creation of City Quay as a separate parish. A new parochial house was built in the following decade.

The Dublin port and docks was a world on its own, filled with transient sailors and ill-paid stevedores. This was a poor parish with many problems in which the comforts of religion played an important role. It was here among the dock workers and carriers that James Larkin and James Connolly laid the foundations of the trade union movement in Ireland. Here the great Lock-out of 1913 laid a heavy hand of suffering on the already impoverished and ill-fed families of the men who followed them.

Dublin is no longer the port it once was, and container freight has ended much of the casual work on the docks which was essential to the district. Many of the warehouses have been converted into newer forms of business, such as television production. People have moved away. But the community still survives, now housed in excellent modern Corporation houses (which are models of their kind). For a period the church itself was under threat of closure. But as the community has survived, so too has the church, which remains a delightful example of its period, past which now roars the full stream of diverted city traffic, making it even more of a contrasting retreat of peace and quiet.

City Quay church exterior.
PHOTO PETER COSTELLO

The Chapel Royal (Most Holy Trinity), Dublin Castle

[FORMERLY CHURCH OF IRELAND, NOW ROMAN CATHOLIC]

There has always been a church in the precincts of Dublin Castle since it was created in Norman times. The old structure was rebuilt in the early eighteenth century, but a scheme for a new chapel having been abandoned later on, it was more or less ruinous by the beginning of the nineteenth century.

The present Chapel Royal was designed by Francis Johnston and was constructed between 1807 and 1814. Gothic revival in style, it is built in black calp limestone, fitted out with the pinnacles and crenellations on the exterior so common on churches of the day. As well there are carvings by Edward Smyth and his son, for instance St Peter and Jonathan Swift on the north door. Inside are the usual galleries common in so many Dublin churches. The pulpit, a richly carved affair, was a main feature of the church. Into the great east window was placed ancient stained glass, distinguished by its archaic figures and deep rich hues, which had been brought from Russia by Lord Whitworth during his years as Viceroy (1813-17).

This is undoubtedly one of Johnston's best works, the splendid black bog-oak carvings, plaster-work, and the fan vaultings being among the finest of their kind. The chapel was used by the Lord Lieutenant for official purposes and as a private chapel, projecting galleries being reserved for his use and that of the Archbishop of Dublin. On panels in the galleries and windows are recorded the arms of the Viceroys since 1172. By a curious chance, the last open space was used for the arms of Lord Fitzalan, the last Viceroy in 1922.

The castle passed to the Irish government in 1922. In 1943 the church was renovated and subsequently used as a Roman Catholic church dedicated to the Most Holy Trinity (which had been invoked in the preamble to the Irish Constitution in 1937). The alterations were made with some sensitivity. The pulpit and the choir stalls, which had been placed centrally, were removed and an altar created in place of the communion table. (The pulpit is now in St Werburgh's close by.) The chapel was much used by the civil servants whose offices surround it. Closed again in recent years because of structural decay, a large sum has been spent to renew the fabric as part of a general overhaul of the castle.

Johnston also rebuilt the Record Tower which abuts the chapel, (its stark plainness contrasting with the fancy decoration of the church), casing it in black calp and adding on the crenellations. The Chapel Royal is only one of the interesting buildings that make up Dublin Castle, the State Apartments now being among the most visited sights in the city.

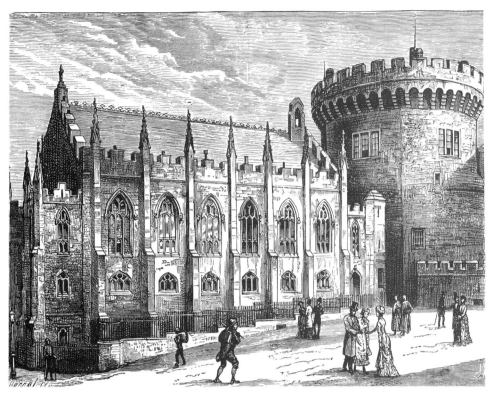

The exterior of the Chapel Royal from an engraving of the 1880s.
AUTHOR'S COLLECTION

A view of the interior.
IRISH ARCHITECTURAL ARCHIVE

College Chapel, Trinity College

[INTERDENOMINATIONAL]

The Chapel was an integral part of the eighteenth-century development of the university, facing as it does the examination hall, making a square with the front buildings which form the familiar façade the university presents to the outside world. The building belongs to the 1760s, and contains some fine carving, notably along the gallery. The plaster-work is by the remarkable Michael Stapleton. There are memorial windows to Bishop Berkeley and Dr Graves, both of which have amusingly appropriate texts.

This was built and long remained an Anglican place of worship. Today the chapel is uniquely interdenominational, and is used by all the churches who maintain a chaplain in the college (the Church of Ireland, the Catholics and the Methodists). There is now a Blessed Sacrament Chapel in a room off the porch of the chapel. In this arrangement perhaps the optimistic might see the hope of the future, with all religions sharing facilities while respecting their own special points of view. The ethos of the college is bound by its old traditions, but is not particularly religious in the way it once was.

Blessed Sacrament Chapel, D'Olier Street

[ROMAN CATHOLIC]

This chapel for the continual exposition of the Blessed Sacrament was blessed and opened by Dr McQuaid, Archbishop of Dublin, in 1970. The building had, however, long been famous as the Red Bank Restaurant. This is briefly featured, like so many Dublin institutions of the day, in the pages of *Ulysses*. On the way to the funeral the carriage travels up D'Olier Street when they pass Blazes Boylan: 'From the door of the Red Bank the white disk of a straw hat flashed reply: spruce figure: passed.' 'The worst man in Dublin', Bloom thinks. The Red Bank was a shoal out in Dublin Bay from which prize oysters were gathered.

This was the slightly racy past of the rooms into which have been fitted a small well-designed chapel, with the altar in the middle flanked by pews in what had been the dining rooms. The effect is much like praying in the Catacombs.

Exterior of the Chapel, Trinity College.
PHOTO PETER COSTELLO

Exterior of the Blessed Sacrament Chapel from D'Olier Street.
PHOTO PETER COSTELLO

St Michan's, Church Street

[CHURCH OF IRELAND]

Dedicated to a Danish saint in 1095, St Michan's was the first church outside the city to be built by the Norse, and for 500 years was the only parish church on the north bank of the Liffey.

The present church dates only from 1685; it was restored in the last century when the main body of the church was demolished and the present building erected, with only the tower (which dates from the twelfth century) surviving from earlier times. The effigy in a niche on the south wall is said to represent St Michan himself. The church plate is of interest, as it includes a silver gilt chalice which dates from 1516.

Though plain enough inside, the high relief carving of musical instruments on the front of the gallery and of fruits and flowers under the organ is remarkably fine — indeed in the past some thought real fiddles had been used.

The church has long been celebrated for its vaults and the mummified remains which can be seen there. Visitors can shake hands with the 'crusader' and another figure said to be a nun. The magnesium salts in the limestone absorb the moisture in the air, leaving the vaults bone dry, and reducing the bodies to leathery bags. But despite the legendary identities of the figures, these vaults date only from the seventeenth century, and the bodies must therefore be those of quite respectable Dublin trades people.

At one time the pathetic body of an infant was displayed, with the faded white ribbons of its funeral dress still on its wrists, the tiny finger and toe nails clearly visible, in a coffin dated 1679. But a visitor stole one of the hands and so the family refused to have the body shown any more.

The Sheares brothers, heroes of the 1798 Rebellion, are also buried in these vaults. Others involved in that Rising, such as Rev. William Jackson and Oliver Bond, are buried here too. A grave in the churchyard was said to be that of Robert Emmet — when opened it contained the remains of a young girl and an old man.

Handel is said to have given the first performance of *Messiah* on the organ (dated 1747) which is claimed to have come from the Fishamble Street hall — though this is disputed. Edmund Burke, author of *Reflections on the French Revolution*, was baptised in the font. The Stool of Repentance, on which parishioners 'who were open and notorious naughty livers' did public penance in more puritanical times, is the only one of its kind still preserved in Dublin.

The tower is 37 metres high and would provide a magnificent view over the city of Dublin if the long and difficult stairs were open to the public.

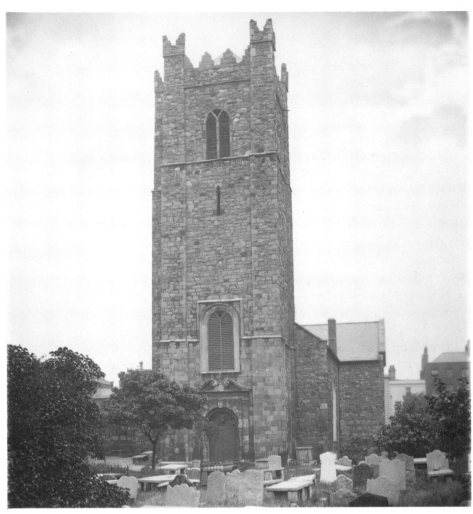

The tower of St Michan's survives from the twelfth century.
LAWRENCE COLLECTION. NATIONAL LIBRARY OF IRELAND

Interior of St Michan's, showing the organ on which Handel is said to have played, and the fine carving on the gallery.
LAWRENCE COLLECTION. NATIONAL LIBRARY OF IRELAND

The mummies in the vaults.
PHOTO BORD FAILTE

Rotunda Hospital Chapel, Parnell Street

[CHURCH OF IRELAND]

The Rotunda Lying-In Hospital was founded by Dr Bartholomew Mosse in 1745, and was the first of its kind in Ireland or Britain. The original premises were in 59 South Great George's Street, but these soon proved too small. Mosse set about raising money for new premises, and hit upon the scheme of using part of his site at Rutland (now Parnell) Square as a pleasure ground where the best in modern music was to be heard. Eventually the Rotunda Theatre itself was erected. In this way the money to pay for the hospital next door was soon in hand.

The Rotunda is built on a lavish scale, and nothing is more lavish than the chapel. The architect was the pre-eminent Richard Cassels (1690-1751), but the real glory of this pillared room is the wood carving by John Kelly and the plaster-work by Barthelemy Cramillion.

The decorations are appropriately all on the theme of motherhood. Above the main window is the figure of Charity as a mother with her children round her. Various texts from the bible, held up by angels, decorate the ceiling, such as that above the font: 'That our sons may grow up as the young plants, and that our daughters may be as the polished corners of the temple.'

The centre of the ceiling was to have been adorned with a painting of the nativity by Cipriani, but this final touch was prevented by the death of Mosse in 1759. The enigmatic Cramillion too left some of his plaster-work incomplete, for he drowned on the voyage back to Ireland from Italy. His achievement is more sculpture than mere plaster-work, for the figures stand out in the highest kind of round relief. Mosse paid him five hundred guineas for the incomparable masterpiece of baroque art.

The chapel is open to visitors on application at the porter's desk in the main entrance to the hospital, and there are regular Sunday services. Both the pleasure ground and the chapel were ancillary to Mosse's true purpose, which was to provide maternity care for the poor of the city. The great medical tradition which he began is still carried on both in the daily work of the hospital and in the teaching and research of the staff. To Mosse might be applied the text on the chapel ceiling: 'Out of the mouths of babes and sucklings has thou perfected praise.'

General view of the interior.
PHOTO IRISH ARCHITECTURAL ARCHIVE

Detail from the interior of the Rotunda Chapel.
PHOTO PETER COSTELLO

Figure above the main window behind the pulpit.
PHOTO PETER COSTELLO

Chapel, Old King's Hospital, Blackhall Place

[ANGLICAN]

The King's Hospital or Blue Coat School was founded in 1662 by Charles II, on the model of Christ's Hospital in London (which educated Lamb and many others). The Blue Coat School owned the land hereabouts in Oxmantown and laid out the neighbouring streets in the plan they still hold. The picture from Brooking's map of Dublin shows the old school before 1728. The boys wore peculiar uniforms, actual blue coats, later changed to military ones, but these were discontinued in 1925. The school has since been removed to an estate in Palmerstown where it has been transformed into a modern co-educational establishment which thrives. The present buildings, designed by Thomas Ivory, were begun in 1773. The first boys were admitted in December 1783. James Malton's aquatint shows the school in the last years of the eighteenth century, with the steeple and cupola which were part of Ivory's plan, but never finished. Though costs prevented the original plans being carried out to their full extent, the result nevertheless was one of the city's finest buildings, consisting of a central range flanked by the dining hall and the chapel.

The Law Society of Ireland, the professional body of Irish solicitors, has occupied these historic premises since 1978, and it is to be hoped that the religious nature of the chapel, now the President's Room, will be recalled from time to time with appropriate services.

The chapel, like the rest of the school, is in the classical style with Corinthian pilasters on the east wall framing a round-headed window in which is a modern stained glass window by Evie Hone of Christ in glory with two angels at his feet. The room has now been redecorated by the Law Society and given a new ceiling.

The chapel in the old days was a cold place, it plainness relieved by a large picture of the Resurrection over the communion table, a very unusual thing indeed to find in any Anglican church or chapel in Ireland.

In the gallery is a bronze memorial framed in wood to the solicitors and solicitors' apprentices killed in the Great War. It shows Victory resting her sword flanked by the thirty-eight names of the dead soldiers. Having survived the destruction of the Law Society's old premises in the Four Courts during the Civil War in 1922, it now adds a suitable touch of piety to an otherwise secularised building.

The Blue Coat School, with the Chapel to the right, about 1792.
PAINTING BY JAMES MALTON. NATIONAL GALLERY OF IRELAND

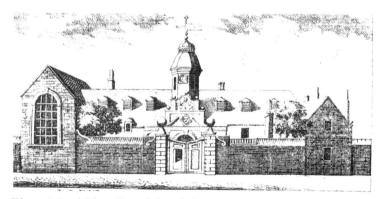

The original Blue Coat School, before 1728.
AUTHOR'S COLLECTION

Modern view of the Chapel interior.
COURTESY INCORPORATED LAW SOCIETY

St Paul's, Arran Quay

[ROMAN CATHOLIC]

St Paul's Catholic parish was created in 1707, being a division made by Archbishop Byrne of the ancient parish of St Michan's, constituted in 1096.

The first chapel was at the rere of 11 Arran Quay, behind the house in which the orator Edmund Burke was born in 1729. In that year the building collapsed, killing several parishioners. The parish priest acted quickly, taking over the site of a neighbouring warehouse on which was erected a small chapel. This was in use into the 1830s, after which it was converted into a wine vault.

The present church, designed by Patrick Byrne, was built in 1835, and dedicated two years later. This is the most central of Byrne's many churches, and he is among the most important architects in the second quarter of the last century. The portico, bell-turret and cupola were additions of 1843. The bells themselves were cast by James Sheridan of Church Street nearby and erected the following year. (For a couple of decades after 1908 a society of change ringers flourished in the parish.)

The painted reredos, *The Conversion of St Paul*, fronted by Corinthian columns and pilasters, dominates the interior, the classical austerity of which is still remarkable.

The church is best seen from the other side of the river, breaking the run of the older Georgian houses along the quays, which these days have lost much of their architectural integrity. The church itself retains its original interest however, and stands out among the wreckage of the older Dublin that surrounds it. The parochial house which was built in the 1920s was set back from the quays, providing an open space on part of which was erected a Lourdes grotto in the 1930s.

Arran Quay was reunited with St Michan's Halston Street in 1974, and the number of services cut sharply by the Capuchin Fathers who have charge of the parish today. The movement of people away from what had been until the 1950s a very densely populated part of Dublin has almost made this fine church redundant. (The parish chapel-of-ease in Cabra, where many had gone to live, was made a separate parish in 1941.) The increase of traffic along the quays now makes access to the church very difficult. Complete closure is still a strong possibility. But nevertheless St Paul's still has its share not only of funerals but also of marriages and baptisms.

St Paul's, Arran Quay, at the turn of the century.
LAWRENCE COLLECTION. NATIONAL LIBRARY OF IRELAND

St Michan's, Halston Street

[ROMAN CATHOLIC]

T his St Michan's is not to be confused with the older church in the same area which passed into Anglican hands in 1562. The century that followed is obscure. About 1682 the parish priest, Dr Cornelius Nary, erected a small chapel in Mary's Lane at Bull Lane as a Catholic parish church. It also served as the Metropolitan Church for the Archbishop of Dublin. It was here that the late medieval statue of Our Lady of Dublin from St Mary's Abbey (now in Whitefriars Street) was preserved. The chapel ended its existence as a school house.

For many centuries St Michan's was the only parish on the north side of the Liffey. In 1707 the new parishes of St Mary and St Paul were created.

This church was built in 1811-14 facing on to North Anne Street, where the original plain gothic façade in granite masonry can still be seen. The perpendicular gothic façade in fussy rustic granite masonry which now fronts the building on Halston Street was built in 1891 to the designs of George Ashlin for Canon Robert Conlan. The contrast between these two faces tells the whole story of the Catholic Church in Dublin during the nineteenth century, a movement from obscure plainness to a dominant extravagance.

The entrance from Halston Street is through the base of the tower. The interior has some interesting stucco work from the early period. The holy-water font comes from the old church and is dated 1707. In the old church there had been a painting of St Francis Xavier. In the new St Michan's there was preserved from penal days a crucifix which had belonged to the saint. It was stolen in 1983.

At the rere of the church is the Presentation Convent which was founded in 1794 and is one of the oldest convents of the Order in Ireland. Facing the church is Green Street Courthouse, the scene of many famous trials in the past, and in which the Special Criminal Court now sits under heavy security. Beside it is the site of the old Newgate prison, now a playground, with a memorial to the United Irishmen of 1798. This area had once been a part of St Mary's Abbey called 'Abbey Green', hence Green Street. Though now less populous than of old, the neighbourhood is brought alive on weekdays by the nearby fruit market with its almost medieval colour.

New façade in Halston Street.
PHOTO PETER COSTELLO

Exterior of old St Michan's, North Anne Street.
PHOTO PETER COSTELLO

St Mary and All Angels, Church Street

[FRANCISCAN CAPUCHIN FATHERS]

This church of the Capuchin Fathers is one of the most popular in Dublin, and is well placed facing out on to Father Mathew Square.

The Capuchins originated as a reformed branch of the Franciscans in 1525, and arrived in Ireland in 1616. After an unsettled existence in Penal times, they came to Church Street in the early eighteenth century. Their chapel there was rebuilt in 1796, and was a simple affair fronting directly on to the street.

Today's church was designed by J.J. McCarthy in what was called decorated gothic, but which has some earlier features. It was begun in 1868 but not completed until 1881. The plan was a simple one with a nave, shallow chancel and porch, but many additions have been made over the years. The gothic style of the exterior with its large lancet and rose windows and canopied statues, the central one of Our Lady, is very impressive, and continues inside with a high altar and decorated apse which are most striking. The inscriptions on the Stations of the Cross are (uniquely for Dublin) in Gaelic only. The side altars are dedicated to St Patrick, St Brigid and St Colmcille.

The open timbered roof has been restored to a very handsome appearance, and though the side aisle (an addition of 1908) has been partitioned off to make a separate Sacred Heart chapel, the church as a whole remains a fine example of its architect's work. The private chapel of the Third Order of St Francis was build in 1891, the gallery and choir loft in 1906, the shrine of St Anthony of Padua in 1945 and the Lourdes grotto in 1950. There are bust portraits of Fr Patrick Reilly, whose drive erected the church, and of Fr Theobald Mathew at the terminals of the chancel arch. Many of the altars and sculptures are the work of James Pearse, the father of Patrick Pearse. The statues of St Francis and St Clare on the front façade are by Leo Broe.

Beside the church is the Father Mathew Hall which commemorates the great Capuchin temperance crusader. The hall and monastery were erected in 1881. It was from this community that for many decades Fr Senan edited the *Capuchin Record*, in which so much fine writing appeared, and which did so much to enhance the appreciation of the graphic arts in Ireland at a bleak period in the cultural life of the country.

The west front of the church today.
PHOTO PETER COSTELLO

Interior of the church about 1914.
AUTHOR'S COLLECTION

Calvary outside the church.
PHOTO PETER COSTELLO

The Holy Family, Aughrim Street

[ROMAN CATHOLIC]

The parish of Aughrim Street was constituted in 1893 from St Paul's, Arran Quay. The church had been built in 1876 as a chapel-of-ease to St Paul's from the designs of J.S. Butler. More work was done at a later date by Doolin, Butler and Donnelly, Butler's firm.

At this period this area of the north side towards the Phoenix Park was being filled in with upper middle-class houses along the North Circular Road and its branches, in a major expansion of the city. Here, however, along Aughrim Street and Prussia Street was a more working-class area. A major feature of the neighbourhood was the military barracks on the other side of the circular road and alongside the riverside. The cattle market to the east also brought a great deal of activity to the area. With the coming of the Free State the civic guards based in the Phoenix Park paraded here on Sundays.

The striking feature of the exterior is the high relief over the main entrance of the Holy Family. The broad and lofty interior uses marbles from various parts of Ireland to splendid decorative effect. The altar of Our Lady is by John Hogan. The interior paintings are the early work of R.M. Butler, later Professor of Architecture at University College Dublin (and the designer of the college building in Earlsfort Terrace). The organ gallery is enhanced by a medieval gothic design. Modernised to the new liturgy, the church retains its character as a later Victorian creation.

In many ways, in its location and design, the Holy Family epitomises Irish churches of the nineteenth century, and though the neighbourhood has seen many changes since the day it was built, the immediate area retains much of the atmosphere of Dublin in 1900.

High relief over the main door of the Holy Family.
PHOTO PETER COSTELLO

Exterior of the Holy Family in Aughrim Street.
PHOTO PETER COSTELLO

Holy Cross, Clonliffe

[ROMAN CATHOLIC]

Founded by Cardinal Cullen in 1879 for the training of priests, Holy Cross College stands in its own extensive grounds on Clonliffe Road. Built in the classical style with a granite façade, the interior follows the style of a Roman basilica, for Cardinal Cullen was eager to emphasise to the world the Roman element in Roman Catholicism.
The decoration, too, owes much to this Roman connection. Between the clerestory windows are eight paintings by Gagliardi, who also executed the Stations of the Cross. The north and south side altars were presented to Dr Cullen by Pius IX.
In the portico are two statues: one of Cardinal Cullen (a copy of the monument by Farrell in the Pro-Cathedral); and another of Pius IX by Matteini of Rome.
Cardinal Cullen, to complete the sense of personal connection with the college, is himself buried in the crypt under the apse. Cullen was the creator of the 'traditional Irish Catholicism' which flourished between the Synod of Thurles in 1850 and the Second Vatican Council.

Corpus Christi, Drumcondra

[ROMAN CATHOLIC]

Though the actual situation on Home Farm Road recalls the more rural history of Drumcondra up to the 1870s, this church belongs resolutely to modern times.
It was designed in 1938 by Robinson, Keefe, and Devane and is among the most important buildings of its period. It is built in granite which, as the local stone of Dublin, has long been the preferred material of local architects.
But it is the actual design that is significant. It follows the tradition of the Roman basilica, which Cullen favoured in his time, but reinterprets it. The external finish owes much to the current vogue for art deco, the influence of which can be seen in the treatment of the actual mass of the church and in the details of the doors and windows.
The interior too is of the highest quality, with an almost scientifically exact purity of conception and line. The sombre yet rich stone-work of the altar and baldacchino are powerfully effective, as is the treatment and finish throughout the work. This is a church filled with Catholic confidence and certainty, a church which reflects the spirit of the Ireland of the Eucharistic Congress and Mr de Valera.

Exterior of Holy Cross College chapel.
PETER COSTELLO

The exterior of Corpus Christi today.
PHOTO PETER COSTELLO

Interior of Corpus Christi.
PHOTO IRISH ARCHITECTURAL ARCHIVE

Our Lady of Dolours, Glasnevin

[ROMAN CATHOLIC]

Better known to many Dubliners as the Church of the Seven Dolours, this parish was created from Fairview in 1912. There had been a wood and iron church here since 1882. There was nothing remarkable about this chapel, for with its simple porch, nave, transept and apse it was a church in miniature. It did stalwart service until the 1960s. By this time expense meant that the vast basilicas of the 1930s were things of the past. The church was replaced with a very modern church, triangular in aspect, which was both pleasing to the eye, simpler to build, and which provided a more intimate atmosphere better suited to the modern liturgy.

This in itself was a transformation. For the nearby Glasnevin Cemetery contains examples of earlier religious building in quite different styles. Thus in one small area can be seen almost the entire gamut of church architecture.

St Joseph's, East Wall

[ROMAN CATHOLIC]

This parish had its beginnings in a chapel-of-ease for Seville Place erected in 1924. This was a 'tin church' of wood and iron at Church Road in the district across the railway tracks to the east of the original parish church. This was in the heart of Dublin's docklands, and the population continued to grow as long as the port of Dublin remained active. Economic change has brought great hardships to this area in recent years, for many of the docks have disappeared or taken on new forms. For many there is an ironic contrast between the international financial centre in the old docks and the needs of the local people.

The parish was created in 1941 when the present church was built. Built in brick in the Romanesque style which was favoured at that time, it is a nice enough building, rather marred by the odd arrangement of the parochial houses to the rere, around a small private piazza. It is solidly surrounded without relief by a dense mass of contemporary Corporation housing. Not perhaps a place for tourists to venture. And in any case the church is often locked.

Our Lady of Dolours, Glasnevin.
PHOTO ROBERT ALLEN

Exterior of St Joseph's.
PHOTO PETER COSTELLO

St Joseph's, Berkeley Road

[ROMAN CATHOLIC]

Originally part of St Michan's parish, a wooden chapel-of-ease was erected in Berkeley Road in 1870. This was replaced by the rustic granite church of St Joseph, designed by O'Neill and Byrne in 1880. The parish was created in 1890, an event marked by the erection of the north-western tower in 1893.

In decorated gothic, the church consists of a nave with side aisles, an apsidal chancel, and several side chapels. The stained glass is fine, with the window at the west end of the Blessed Virgin aisle being by Hardman. The reredos with the 'life-size' angels was the work of Miss Mary Redmond, a Dublin artist who also created the well-known statue of Fr Mathew in O'Connell Street. The adaptations to the new liturgy, which involve an apron sanctuary and cast enamel decorations, are on the over-modern side for a church that contains so much Victorian gothic work.

Across the road stands the bulk of the Mater Hospital, which had been founded in 1861. The design was by John Bourke. Over the years the hospital and its private wing took over the whole of the north side of Eccles Street, eventually engulfing even No. 7 in which Joyce had placed the home of Leopold and Molly Bloom. (In his lifetime it had been the sometime residence of his close friend J.F. Byrne.) A new private nursing home on the site was opened in 1985.

The neighbourhood consists mostly of small two-storey late Victorian houses in a warm red brick of the kind ubiquitous in the outer regions of inner Dublin. Here, where many of the streets are in good condition, they make a very attractive foil to the solid bulk of the church and the hospital.

In the park alongside the church is a monument to the Irish historians of the seventeenth century, the Four Masters. This was put up 1872 through the enthusiasm of William Martin Murphy, that great entrepreneur whose name has been soiled by the events of 1913. It commemorates Brother Michael O'Clery and his colleagues who laboured in the Franciscan monastery in Donegal through the years 1632-6 to preserve the materials on Irish history which they had gleaned on their travels through Ireland. Their annals were a landmark in Irish historiography, as seen from the Catholic point of view. Hence the erection of this monument at the moment when the tide of modern Irish nationalism was on the rise.

Monument to the Fourt Masters with St Joseph's in the background.
PHOTO PETER COSTELLO

St Joseph's, Berkeley Road, about 1932.
AUTHOR'S COLLECTION

Shrine of Our Lady.
PHOTO PETER COSTELLO

St Peter's Church, Phibsborough

[ROMAN CATHOLIC]

The first church on this site, where the Cabra Road and the North Circular Road come together, was opened in 1831 when this was a semi-rural area, where four parishes met.

The name is derived from the Phipps family who were the local landlords. The construction in the 1790s of the Royal Canal, that ringed Georgian Dublin to the north, brought with it a rise in population.

It was to serve the needs of this isolated community that a committee was formed in 1826 to raise money for a building that would double as a school and a church. The result was a simple though attractive building in the classical mode of the period, but without the tower.

The chapel was taken over by the Vincentian Order in 1838, when it was extended. The present church and community house, however, are the end result of a long era of building and rebuilding.

In 1862 the superior, then a Fr McNamara, observing the growth of the city around him, thought it was due time to improve upon the original edifice. The present sanctuary and transepts, designed by Goldie, Child and Goldie, were completed in 1869. The central tower which had been a feature of this building had later to be taken down — the stone going towards the construction of a local public house. The nave was completely rebuilt to the designs of Ashlin and Coleman in 1902-7. The spectacular spire, which is more than 200 feet high and the highest in the city, was erected at this time.

The final result was a building in decorated gothic on the scale of a small cathedral. The church was much admired when it opened, particularly the High Altar, the fifteen side chapels and several of the transept windows, all of which were conceived as part of a grand design, especially in the use of a great variety of marbles.

This neighbourhood along the North Circular Road and the Cabra Road was developed from 1860 onwards. The great feature of the neighbourhood was the cattle market into which the cattle from the country were brought by drovers, often from as far as Connaught, and from which the herds were driven down the streets to the docks for export. The pathetic sight of these animals was the subject of literary reflection by both Joyce and Sean O'Casey.

Otherwise this was a respectable neighbourhood, as the roads on towards the Phoenix Park suggest, providing both the people and the funds to support the building of this magnificent church. Though the neighbourhood had declined socially since then, the population has increased, and in 1974 St Peter's was constituted as a separate parish.

The landmark spire of St Peter's, 200 feet high, photographed in the 1950s.
AUTHOR'S COLLECTION

St Saviour's, Dominick Street

[DOMINICAN FATHERS]

The Dominicans have been in Dublin since 1124. Their original priory was on the site of the Four Courts and was confiscated at the time of the Reformation. After that they led a fugitive existence (for the Orders as against registered priests were banned under the Penal Laws), first at Bridge Street on the south side of the river until they moved in 1772 to Denmark Street on the north side, where they stayed till the 1860s. This present church was built on the site of an abandoned coach factory beside what had been the Dublin Penitents Retreat. The architect chosen was J.J. McCarthy, and this building has been described by Jeanne Sheehy in her study of his work as 'the most important of [his] city churches'.

The foundation stone was laid in 1852 and the church dedicated in 1861. It had a not untroubled history and was finally left unfinished. The front façade which is the most visible part of the exterior is weakened by this fact, but the interior with its high arches, delicate tracery and carving is very fine, and for many Dubliners it is the most beautiful church in the city. The south aisle is a later addition. To conform to the new liturgy the fine Caen stone altar and the gothic reredos have been removed, but elsewhere the church retains its original atmosphere.

Under the Holy Name altar is a panel by John Hogan, *The Dead Christ*. In the south aisle one of the stained glass windows was erected by Earl Spencer to commemorate Mr Burke, the Under-Secretary murdered by the terrorist group the Invincibles in the Phoenix Park in 1882.

It was on the rere approach to the church, in Granby Row, that Matt Talbot collapsed and died in June 1925, thus revealing an extraordinary life of prayer and penance which has been found both controversial and edifying.

The Dominican priory alongside the church and running back to Dorset Street was designed by J.L. Robinson in 1885 and worked on for several decades. It makes a pleasant oasis in this decayed area of Dublin which dates back to the 1720s. Many of the eighteenth-century houses, some of which contained some of the best period plaster-work in the city, have been swept away to be replaced by Corporation flats.

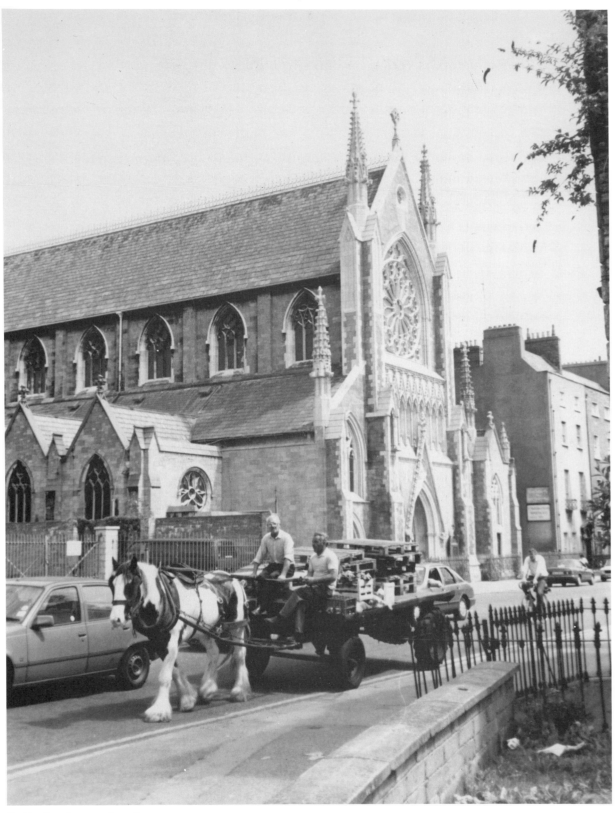

St Saviour's west façade.
PHOTO PETER COSTELLO

St Agatha's, North William Street

[ROMAN CATHOLIC]

Originally part of the parish of the pro-Cathedral, this area was served for many years by the chapel of the convent in North William Street. In 1853 it was made a parish, but it was not until 1908 that this church, designed by William H. Byrne, was dedicated. This was in a classical Roman style more akin to the churches of the early nineteenth century than to the more recent gothic ones.

Erected on a narrow city site, the façade is perhaps difficult to appreciate. The pediment is crowned by statues of the Sacred Heart, St Patrick and St Agatha, a Sicilian virgin of the third century who was canonised for her 'indomitable chastity'. The church, too, is chaste, depending on its architectural features for decoration. In the arches of the apse are three large paintings of *The Agony in the Garden, The Supper at Emmaus,* and *The Annunciation.* The Stations of the Cross, placed in the other arches, are by the Dublin artist Charles Goodland Bradshaw.

St Francis Xavier's, Gardiner Street

[JESUIT FATHERS]

On the return of the Jesuits to Ireland a city church was among their first plans. St Francis Xavier's was begun in 1829 and finished in 1832. It was designed by John B. Keane of Mabbot Street. The Ionic portico, though impressive, blends well with the Georgian houses between which it was built. Inside, a feature of the nave is the coffered ceiling. The chapel of St Ignatius, the founder of the Jesuits, was added in 1850 and enlarged at a later date. In the northern side chapel is the tomb of Fr John Sullivan, the saintly Jesuit whose canonisation is now being actively pursued.

The paintings in the nave by Gagliardi illustrate episodes from the lives of the early saints of the Society of Jesus.

This is one of the city's finest churches and has always had a special place in the religious life of the northside. It was a church familiar to the Jesuit-educated Joyce who uses it as the setting for the businessmen's retreat in his short story *Grace,* a fiction redolent of his knowledge of the religious life of Dublin in the 1890s.

St Agatha's shortly after it opened.
LAWRENCE COLLECTION. NATIONAL LIBRARY OF IRELAND

St Joseph's altar in Gardiner Street Church about 1900.
AUTHOR'S COLLECTION

The tomb of Fr John Sullivan.
PHOTO PETER COSTELLO

Exterior of St Francis Xavier's.
PHOTO PETER COSTELLO

St Thomas's, Cathal Brugha Street

[CHURCH OF IRELAND]

The original Church of Ireland parish church stood in Marlborough Street. It was designed by John Smith and built in 1758-62. The parish had been created in 1749. At that date the church looked out over fields, but with the development of Gloucester Street the church was taken up into the city fabric. The façade was modelled after Palladio's Venetian Redentore, but was left incomplete and rather ugly. The interior had a compartmented ceiling and a gallery raised on Ionic columns. The severity of the design was softened in late Victorian times by some High Church painting by Messrs Sibthorpe, who added texts to the walls.

During the Civil War in 1922 the church, along with a large area of O'Connell Street, was completely destroyed. In the rebuilding an opportunity was taken to drive Gloucester Street through into O'Connell Street, creating Cathal Brugha Street (named after the Irregular leader who had died in the street fighting there).

The present little brick church in the Byzantine style was designed by Frederick Hicks in 1931 (and received a RIAA medal in 1932). Some of the monuments from the old church can be found to the left of the entrance. St Thomas's is unusual in having a Dublin working-class congregation. Originally the church stood among houses, but now is towered over by new office developments to which its tree-shaded enclosure makes a peaceful contrast.

St Thomas's today.
PHOTO PETER COSTELLO

Rere of St Thomas's.
PHOTO PETER COSTELLO

Our Lady of Lourdes, Sean MacDermott Street

[ROMAN CATHOLIC]

This area was on the edge of the notorious Monto, the Nightown of Joyce's *Ulysses*, and a more unsavoury quarter existed in few other cities. The prostitution was only one aspect of a well-documented history of poverty and privations, which has still to be lifted, despite the efforts of modern planners and their eager partners, the politicians. Critics in the nineteenth century often wondered aloud how such things could exist only a short step from the Pro-Cathedral, and what was the involvement of Catholic city fathers in local property. Many of the old houses and streets have simply been swept away, and Gloucester Street, the heart of the red-light district, has been renamed after the patriot Sean MacDermott.

There was for a long time a 'tin church' here, but in 1954 a new church was built, the parish being created in 1970. This large modern-style building contrasts with the surrounding Georgiana and the open areas of Corporation demolition on which future developments will spring up. The church contains the shrine of Matt Talbot, to whom many of his fellow-Dubliners have a strong devotion, and the large size of the church, far beyond the needs of the immediate parish, was intended by Dr McQuaid to cope with what he foresaw as a growing pilgrimage to the tomb of this unique Dublin saint. Matt Talbot's life has been the subject both of foolish piety and ill-directed criticism. He was for much of his life a worker in Brooks Thomas's woodyard, and a trade union member. The chronicle of his life of drink, hardship, poverty and prayer is a revelation of the social and emotional conditions under which Dubliners lived in the 'rare ould days'. Renaming the street after patriots has done little for his class.

Though the surroundings are brutally depressing, the church itself (despite some graffiti on the outside) is a very fine piece of neo-Romanesque work in red brick, with a well-lit interior and nice finishing touches, especially in the use of mosaic work to contrast with the brick. The modernisations for the new liturgy have been carried out with equal style. As the main feature of the church, the tomb of Matt Talbot is a granite mausoleum plainly finished on a slight dais, effective because it is simple. And, as Archbishop McQuaid rightly expected, the pilgrims are already coming.

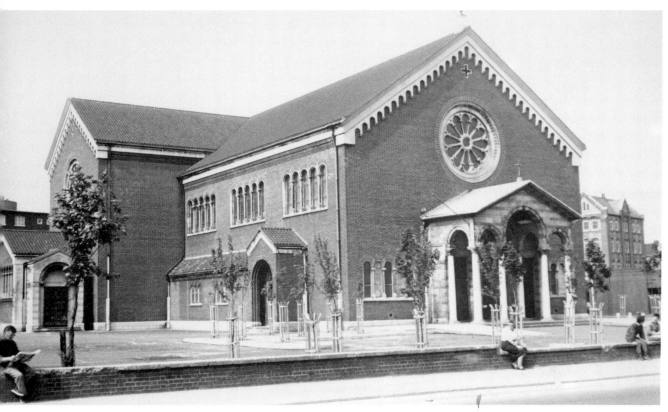

Exterior of Our Lady of Lourdes.
PHOTO PETER COSTELLO

The tomb of Matt Talbot.
PHOTO PETER COSTELLO

St Laurence O'Toole, Seville Place

[ROMAN CATHOLIC]

Sited on a prominent corner where Seville Place meets Sheriff Street, the spire of St Laurence O'Toole towers over its dockland neighbourhood. A fine building of limestone, it was erected in 1850, in early English gothic designed by J.B. Keane. The tower is the work of John Bourke.

The area was part of St Mary's Pro-Cathedral parish until 1852, so the church opened as a chapel-of-ease. It is 150 feet long and 75 feet across the transepts, a huge size. The gothic style is continued in the interior. Above and behind the high altar are statues of St Patrick and St Laurence, the patron saint of Dublin. The altar of 1850 was presented to the church by the clergy of Dublin to mark the significance of the fact that this was the first church in Dublin to be dedicated to the saint. The sanctuary lamp was also presented to the church by a Fr Laurence O'Toole of Manchester.

The church has also a shrine to St Laurence in which a relic of the saint is venerated. This was erected in 1914. It is a phlange (a small bone of the hand or foot) and was brought to Dublin by Archdeacon Brady in the summer of 1914 from Eu in Normandy where the saint had died in 1180 while on his way to Rome. Other relics of the saint exist in Dublin: his heart in Christ Church; a phlange in the convent of the Sisters of Charity in Seville Place (founded 1882); and another bone in the private chapel of the Catholic Archibishop.

The parish houses and the school buildings (dating from 1847) which lie behind the church are all well built, as are the houses that lie along Seville Place. But this is a neighbourhood which has suffered much from being isolated between the railway lines and the river. It is a notoriously tough quarter of the city, where it is not uncommon to see stolen cars being burnt out in the middle of the road, where the police themselves do not care to venture, and where the activities of a few cast a slur over a whole community. This may change with the advent of the financial centre on the old Port and Docks site to the east. A scheme to remove the people from the flats in Sheriff Street in order to demolish the latter met with stiff resistance early in 1989. So it may be that the aspirations of the church towards finer things may yet be reflected in the actual life of the local people.

St Laurence O'Toole's viewed from Sheriff Street.
PHOTO PETER COSTELLO

Abbey Presbyterian Church, Parnell Square

[PRESBYTERIAN CHURCH IN IRELAND]

The Abbey Presbyterian Church was completed in 1864 on the site of Bective House. The congregation paid £2,600 in 1862 for this situation, but the building of the church was paid for by Alex Findlater, the Dublin merchant (whose shops in O'Connell Street and Rathmines were well-known until recently). Hence it has come to be known to Dubliners as 'Findlater's Church'.

The original Presbyterian congregation in Dublin met in Bull Alley in 1661, removing to St Mary's Abbey in 1667, under the Rev. Mr William Jacque. This building had been the one great church building on the north side of the Liffey until the Reformation. All that survives of it now is the Chapter House, in the care of the Board of Works, which can be visited in Meeting House Lane. The Presbyterian chapel was north of this along the same lane, with an entrance from Capel Street. This congregation was unique in that at all times it has been united to the Synod of Ulster. The title of Mary's Abbey was adopted in 1778. Following upon difficulties with their landlord, Sir Jervis White, the congregation moved to Rutland Square (as it then was) in 1864. The historic name of the old congregation was carried over to the new church. The architect of this gothic wonder was Andrew Heiton. The front on to the square with its tower, its slender spire and graceful east window is fine enough, but the range along Frederick Street (which had been set out in 1795) reveals the true grandeur of the building. It represents a triumph of industry and faith in God's special grace which many would think typical of the Presbyterian outlook. It now serves much of north Dublin and, the spire having been recently repaired, would seem to have a long life before it.

There had been a Presbyterian Union Chapel in Gloucester Street, which had been built in the Greek style in 1834 for another Presbyterian tradition going back to 1733 ('The First Secession') who had also met for the previous decade in St Mary's Abbey. Their chapel was destroyed in the Easter Rising and the congregation united with the Abbey Church in 1918.

Abbey Church, Parnell Square façade.
PHOTO PETER COSTELLO

The Scot's Church, Lower Abbey Street

[PRESBYTERIAN CHURCH IN IRELAND]

This church represents the union of two congregations, that of Ormond Quay (closed in 1938) and the original Scot's Church group.

The very name suggests the origins of Presbyterian worship in Ireland as Ulster and Scottish. It was a faith largely of the Dublin banking and business classes, usually those with connections with the North. This church was built from a desire to establish in Dublin a Scottish church for the Scots. In 1863 ministers from the United Presbyterian Church began giving services in the Rotunda. The Abbey Church was eventually opened in 1869. Then in 1900, following upon the union of the United Presbyterian Church with the Free Church of Scotland, the congregation became part of the United Free Church. Eventually joining the Presbyterian Church in Ireland, the congregation retained the title of 'The Scot's Church'.

Methodist City Mission, Lower Abbey Street

[METHODIST CHURCH IN IRELAND]

The apparent upper-class nature of Methodism in Dublin (represented in many minds by Wesley College) hides the fact that originally it was in essence a lower middle-class, upper working-class, dissenting chapel movement. It belonged to the poorer folk. That was where John Wesley found his audience and that was where the Methodists in Dublin long laboured.

In Abbey Street the Mission is in a building which consists of the main church (which was founded in 1820 and rebuilt in 1901), a plain pillared hall, the old galleries of which have been converted into a small chapel (created in 1963) and a coffee shop. Aside from the usual Sunday services, the church also caters for alcoholics and others, coping with all the usual problems faced by all religious groups on the streets of Dublin. Indeed there is some activity there every night. The Methodists today lay a special emphasis on 'social outreach' as an important part of the tradition they have inherited from Wesley and the early Methodists.

The Scot's Church in Abbey Street.
PHOTO PETER COSTELLO

Interior of Methodist Church.
PHOTO PETER COSTELLO

The Methodist Church in Abbey Street.
PHOTO PETER COSTELLO

Fairview Gospel Hall, Annesley Bridge Road

[EVANGELICAL CHRISTIAN]

This is one of the oldest of eight gospel halls in Dublin, and dates from 1912. Placed as an integral part of a development of typical red brick houses of the same period, it is a part of its townscape in a way which many other chapels and churches are not. It is in plain brick with a course of decorated bricks under the eaves, but in its simplicity is an attractive building.

St John the Baptist, Seafield Road, Clontarf

[CHURCH OF IRELAND]

Designed by Joseph Welland, the architect to the Ecclesiastical Commissioners, and his partner Gillespie, St John's was built in 1866, when Clontarf was being developed into a largely upper middle-class residential area from what had been a series of scattered hamlets. The rustic granite building is in the cruciform early English style which was popular with the Commissioners. The tower, placed at an angle to the body of the church, forms a porched entrance. The spire which is such a feature of the church is 45 metres high. The chancel is a later addition.

St Anthony's, Clontarf Road

[ROMAN CATHOLIC]

The history of the Catholic Church in Dublin is expressed in miniature in the churches of Clontarf. The first church was that of St John the Baptist on the Clontarf Road, opened in 1835. In 1895 this was enlarged by the addition of a chancel, sacristy and belfry, designed by Patrick Byrne. Clontarf was made into a parish in 1829.
In 1927 the former Clontarf Town Hall (which had not been used as such since the 1890s) was converted under the supervision of J.J. Robinson into a church dedicated to St Anthony. This in turn was replaced by a church of modern design in 1975, built directly behind it.

Fairview Gospel Hall from Fairview Park.
PHOTO PETER COSTELLO

Exterior of St Anthony's, Clontarf.
PHOTO PETER COSTELLO

St John's church in Seafield Road.
PHOTO PETER COSTELLO

War memorial at St John's, Seafield Road.
PHOTO PETER COSTELLO

Raheny Parish Churches

[ROMAN CATHOLIC AND CHURCH OF IRELAND]

Raheny village presents the vistor with an example of church development of great historical interest. In Gaelic Rath Enna, Enna's fort, the remains of the old defense work can be seen around the old Anglican church in Main Street, itself built on a medieval site.

St Assam's Roman Catholic Church, which stands on the south corner of Main Street, was erected in 1864 to the design of Patrick Byrne. A small church with a simple nave and chancel, it was found too small for a developing area, and a new church was opened on the other side of the street in 1962. But whereas the earlier church is an attractive piece of community architecture, the new church (designed by Peppard and Duffy) dominates in an ugly way not only its ancestor but the whole village. The most charming feature of the immediate area is a crescent row of alms cottages, with which it jars dreadfully.

The exterior is of reinforced concrete faced on the tower and front façade with green limestone. The main entrance was inspired by the door of Clonfert Cathedral, the kind of specious 'Celtic' reference which irritates more than it could ever have pleased. The gloomily high interior continues the restless appearance of the exterior with wavy walls and vile decorations. This most unattractive church is relieved only by a series of very fine handcarved wooden statues. Our Lady of Divine Grace is the sort of church in which we must remind ourselves that prayer is valid wherever it is said.

Further back along Howth Road stands the Anglican All Saints. The site for the church was given by Edmund Guinness, the owner of St Anne's estate nearby (now a public park).

It was designed by George Ashlin, Pugin's son-in-law and a noted Catholic architect. Built of granite with limestone dressings, it uses the Caen stone beloved of High Church architects inside. This is a much larger church than St Assam's, with a nave, transepts, chancel, rounded apse and 34-metre spire. No expense was spared on the materials or the finish, and the detailing of the work both inside and out is remarkable. It has lovely stained glass, the original lighting fixtures and pews, and a cool religious atmosphere. Under the church is a crypt in which are laid to rest Lord and Lady Ardilaun, those great Guinness benefactors to whom the city of Dublin owes St Stephen's Green and much else; aside from stout. A victim of petty vandals, this most beautiful of churches should be better known to Dubliners.

Exterior of the new parish church at Raheny: the tower and elaborate façade are in a greenish limestone.
PHOTO PETER COSTELLO

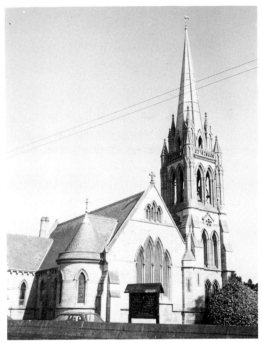

Exterior of All Saints, Raheny, showing the fine finish.
PHOTO PETER COSTELLO

St Assam's, the former Catholic parish church at Raheny Cross.
PHOTO PETER COSTELLO

The tombs of Lord and Lady Ardilaun in the crypt under All Saints.
PHOTO PETER COSTELLO

St Fintan's, Sutton

[ROMAN CATHOLIC]

Since the war and the building of the James Larkin Road, the north shore of the bay has seen a huge expansion along the shore from Clontarf to Howth, with new estates at Bayside and Kilbarrack.

St Fintan's is one of the new churches built to cater for these 'New Dubliners' as a social scientist dubbed them in the 1960s. Designed by Robinson, Keefe and Devane, it was erected in 1973, and is one of the more attractive of the 'new churches'.

It is fronted by an atrium paved with Liscannor stone in which the church tower is located, which acts as a transition from the outside to the interior of the church. The plan is fan-shaped, with the roof rising to the crown of the sanctuary which is lit through slats from above. The Stations of the Cross are engraved on to the side windows in a novel treatment. With its copper roof and ribbed concrete walls, the church is well set in its sea-side site.

The Assumption, Howth

[ROMAN CATHOLIC]

In the centre of Howth village are the remains of St Mary's Abbey, which was in use as an Anglican church into the eighteenth century. Below it stands the Church of the Assumption, a church built at the turn of the century to the design of Patrick Byrne, to replace a smaller chapel. In that Romanesque style which was so popular for Catholic churches at the time, it was completed some years later by the addition of a spire.

Near the village is the St Lawrence estate of Howth Castle where the bells of the abbey are preserved, along with the famous sword of Sir Armoricus Tristram (Joyce's 'violer d'amores' in the opening of *Finnegans Wake*).

All these are indications of the ancient importance of Howth, but it is largely a modern village dating from the end of the eighteenth century, which thrives today as a fishing and sailing centre. Along the hill behind the church are strung out new housing developments for city commuters.

114

St Fintan's church in Sutton.
PHOTO PETER COSTELLO

The front of the church from the village street.
PHOTO PETER COSTELLO

The Assumption viewed from the summit of Howth.
AUTHOR'S COLLECTION

The front door of the church with an untypical parishioner.
PHOTO PETER COSTELLO

St Mary's, Howth

[CHURCH OF IRELAND]

The attractions of Howth (which had been the packet boat station for Dublin between 1807 and 1821) did not develop until the second half of the nineteenth century. It was the arrival of the railway in 1844 that raised the place from being little more than a squalid fishing village.

St Mary's which stands on an elevated site at the entrance to Howth Castle and the St Lawrence estate, was built to cater for this new population seeking the refreshment of the sea air. For many years now it has been the living of Canon Blennerhassett, one of the more colourful members of the Anglican clergy, who serves about 300 families. Built in 1866 in a suitably rustic granite masonry, the church is situated in a lovely position with the new school that is attached to it discretely tucked in at the back. The architect was J.E. Rogers, a pupil of Benjamin Woodward, who saw the style as thirteenth-century English. While the detailing is simple, the unusual treatment of the spire makes an attractive feature, as do the well-kept grounds with their rose bushes and lush trees. On the inside the use of red and yellow bricks with polished marble creates a polychromatic effect.

St Columba's, Iona Road

[ROMAN CATHOLIC]

Built in 1906 at the same time as this area between Prospect Cemetery and the Drumcondra Road was being developed, the dedication of this church derives from the historical association of St Columba or Columcille with this area of north Dublin. The parish was a creation of 1902 from Berkeley Road.

Designed by George Ashlin, the style is a modernised Romanesque, and inside the decorations have also an early Irish or Celtic, or perhaps late Norman, feel. This is emphasised by the 'round tower' at the south-west corner. The stained glass windows in the rounded apse symbolising the Seven Sacraments are particularly notable.

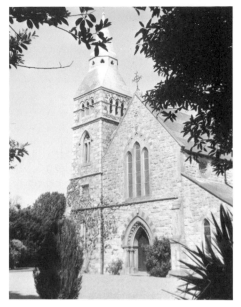

View of the main entrance.
PHOTO PETER COSTELLO

St Mary's just outside Howth.
PHOTO PETER COSTELLO

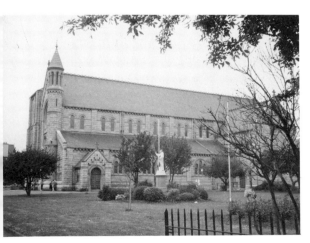

The south range of St Columba's in Iona Road.
PHOTO PETER COSTELLO

The north façade of St Columba's.
PHOTO PETER COSTELLO

St Alphonsus' Monastery, Iona Road
[REDEMPTORISTINE NUNS]

The monastery of St Alphonsus was founded in 1859, in what was semi-urban countryside. The Redemptoristine community which now numbers only eighteen is an enclosed one, the members of which devote themselves to a life of reparation and intercessionary prayer, and also to the making of rosary beads.

The chapel, which is open only for morning Mass and afternoon benediction, was designed by George Ashlin, in the late Norman Romanesque style. Much admired when it was opened, it remains a handsome building of historical interest.

The interior is also very fine with its Bossi work — marble inlaid with coloured cements. But the chapel is only a small, public part of the much larger, and totally private establishment of the monastery itself.

Holy Child, Whitehall
[ROMAN CATHOLIC]

Built in the year 1957 at a cost of £170,000, this church is among the best of its period. The architects were J.J. Robinson and his partner F. Brown of Robinson, Keefe and Devane.

The fine brick-work, which echoes the building material of the surrounding houses, is still good. The campanile is impressive with its copper dome, though the Roman tiles on the connecting passage strike a slightly odd note in the bleak Irish climate.

The interior is also very fine. Plain but well appointed originally, it has been maintained in high order. Over the transept crossing are striking plaster medallions of the Four Evangelists. The new altar area has been created in the same light, honey-coloured marble with which the columns of the church are built, achieving a successful transition between old and new.

A Madonna and Child after Murillo, presented in 1983 to Bishop James Kavanagh (parish priest since 1976), hangs in the south transept, and strikes a happy note in an otherwise largely undecorated interior. Over the main door is a fine mosaic.

Exterior of the chapel of St Alphonsus with its elaborate west window.
PHOTO PETER COSTELLO

Exterior of The Holy Child, Whitehall.
PHOTO PETER COSTELLO

St John the Evangelist, Coolock

[CHURCH OF IRELAND]

Dating from 1760, this church preserves the plain simplicity typical of rural Irish churches of the period. The pinnacles, which were such a feature of late Georgian churches, are here restrained to mere peaks on the square entrance tower, which dates from 1791. Coolock was rural until quite recently which accounts for the unaltered state of the church. But these days local vandals have overturned stones in the graveyard, scrawling them and the walls of the church with Fascist and Satanic symbols. These antisocial acts may sound shocking, but they are not new, for when the church was built the area was notorious for its highwaymen preying on the stagecoaches to the north. As late as 1828 there was a shooting affray between police who had arrested a robber and a gang trying to rescue him at Coolock Bridge.

Our Lady, Queen of Heaven, Dublin Airport

[ROMAN CATHOLIC]

This small church has the distinction of being the first church that visitors arriving in Ireland will see, and also of being the first modern church in the Dublin region when it opened in 1964. It is lucky then that it is one of the finer examples of its kind, the work of Robinson, Keefe and Devane.

It was built to serve the needs of those working at the airport, a large enough congregation, but it is also popular for weddings. The entrance is through a shaded atrium which recalls a medieval cloister. The church itself is in a rectangle in plain grey brick with a large use of natural wood. The interior is restful and unhectic, in contrast to much modern design, lit largely by stained glass clerestory windows. The bell-tower is in cast, self-finished white concrete, not alas the best material for the Dublin climate. The decorations and statuary are by Helen Moloney, Sheila Corcoran and Oisin Kelly.

The tower of St John's, Coolock.
PHOTO PETER COSTELLO

Atrium of Our Lady, Queen of Heaven.
PHOTO PETER COSTELLO

Our Lady of Consolation, Donnycarney
[ROMAN CATHOLIC]

For many years this parish (created from Marino in 1952) was served by a 'tin church'. Though Collins Avenue on which it stands was laid out in the late 1920s, the houses here belong mainly to the late 1940s.

The permanent church was erected in the early 1970s. It is a large cruciform building, with cast concrete piers and brick curtain walls, lit by full-length windows with abstract stained glass, and handbeaten copper doors with New Testament scenes. Though a solid modern building, these details make the church humanly attractive. A recent visit, however, found the church locked, and graffiti, mainly by young lovers, scrawled upon the exterior concrete.

These facts express profoundly the great social change that is sweeping over parts of the city. Once it would have been unthinkable for a church to be vandalised. But now it seems that for some of the younger generation religion has lost its emotional force. The locked door is the church protecting itself from a world that no longer welcomes it with an open heart.

St Columcille's, Swords
[ROMAN CATHOLIC]

The Catholic parish of Swords was created in 1608. This is not surprising, for Swords was always an important place from the earliest days, as the round tower and bishop's palace testify. Tradition records its foundation by St Columcille himself. The complete round tower stands as a relic of the old monastic settlement. The ancient church was rebuilt in the early nineteenth century for Anglican use.

In contrast to these distinguished and ancient buildings, the Catholic church is an attractive late Georgian edifice, inside which can be found a tablet recording the names of the parish priests from the foundation of the parish. The interior itself is plain enough, with a small gallery and round-headed windows.

Front of Our Lady of Consolation from Collins Avenue.
PHOTO PETER COSTELLO

Contrast in art: the handbeaten door of Our Lady of Consolation, and juvenile graffiti.
PHOTO PETER COSTELLO

St Columcille's church in Swords.
PHOTO PETER COSTELLO

St Matthew's Royal Chapel, Irishtown Road
[CHURCH OF IRELAND]

This is one of the new churches actually built early in the eighteenth century following on a church building act of the Irish Parliament. It was erected for the Corporation in 1704-6 in local black calp in what Maurice Craig refers to as 'a quasi-gothic style'. The tower was added later, in 1713.

In 1878-9 the church was demolished and rebuilt by the architect J.F. Fuller, leaving only the tower surviving from the earlier work. When St Matthew's was built, Ringsend was the place where the English packet boat came in, mooring below the Pigeon House (then an hotel) and the fishing village was a picturesque place of some importance, much frequented by Dubliners and the garrison as a summer resort with pretty vine-covered cottages along the sea front. It was for the mariners and fishermen that the church was built, for the village was quite isolated then by the unwalled rivers Liffey and Dodder.

St Mary's, Haddington Road
[ROMAN CATHOLIC]

Originally part of the old rambling parish of Donnybrook and Irishtown, Haddington Road became a separate parish on the erection of St Mary's in 1839. The first church was simple in style, even to having an unpaved earth floor. Improvements were made in 1879, when the rounded apse and the altar (designed by C. Geoghegan) were added. The imposing façade and round belfry, together with the side aisles (designed by J.J. O'Callaghan) and the tower (the work of W.G. Doolin), were built in 1894. The school building to the rere of the church, in St Mary's Road, was the work of J.J. McCarthy in 1870. During the nineteenth century this was one of the wealthiest Catholic parishes in Dublin, as this large amount of building and rebuilding suggests. The parish is perhaps unique in having had a long line of bishops as parish priest, including the scholar and art connoisseur, Dr Donnelly (to whom every writer on the parishes of Dublin is indebted). His memorial can be seen on the north wall of the nave. Opposite it is a memorial to parishioners who fell in the Great War, a memorial unique in Dublin, perhaps even in Irish Catholic churches, and an indication of the solid Unionist views of the parish even in the early days of the Free State.

Detail of St Matthew's front door.
PHOTO PETER COSTELLO

Tower and exterior of St Matthew's, Irishtown.
PHOTO PETER COSTELLO

Exterior of St Mary's.
PHOTO COURTESY DM PHOTOGRAPHY

Eastern aspect of the church showing the earlier, simpler work.
PHOTO PETER COSTELLO

Christ Church, Leeson Park

[CHURCH OF IRELAND/METHODIST]

Leeson Park was a development of the 1860s, with Dartmouth Square being laid out in 1880. The Molyneaux Home for the Female Blind was removed from Peter Street to this then suburban site in 1862 (see p.222), and the church was built to serve both them and the new parish. The architect was Dubliner Rawson Carroll.

For nearly a century this was a very strong community (which even had a chapel-of-ease, St Columba's, and a national school in Ranelagh). The inevitable decline in numbers was stayed by the arrival of the Methodists who, having lost their church in Stephen's Green in a fire, moved here in the 1970s, and built the modernist Wesley Centre behind the quaint Litton Hall (1877). The war memorial outside the church is dated to 1919 — an unusual exactness. Inside, the decoration of the apse (by Sibthorpes) is elaborate in the High Victorian manner, though the tone is distinctly lower than at nearby Clyde Road. Aside from local memorials, the church also contains the tablets removed from St Columba's when it closed.

St Bartholomew's Church, Clyde Road

[CHURCH OF IRELAND]

The parish of St Bartholomew's was constituted in 1864 from the two neighbouring parishes of St Peter and St Mary, Donnybrook. The immediate area of 'The Roads' was being developed at this time and the church was an integral part of this. The architect was Thomas Henry Wyatt, described by John Betjeman as 'one of the dullest Victorian architects'. This church is far from dull, though much of its interest lies in the wonderful decorative work of Sir Thomas Deane around the sanctuary. A Catholic church by conviction, the liturgical and musical traditions are strong here, and charges of ritualism had to be defended in the past. During the Rising two soldiers were buried for a time in the grounds; later the priest prayed for Erskine Childers after his execution in the nearby barracks. The Vicarage (1872 by J.E. Rogers) with its octagonal hall was sold to the Knights of Malta in the 1960s. In the garden is a water fount from St John's Well, Kilmainham which was brought from St James's Church in 1971.

Exterior of Christ Church, Leeson Park.
PHOTO PETER COSTELLO

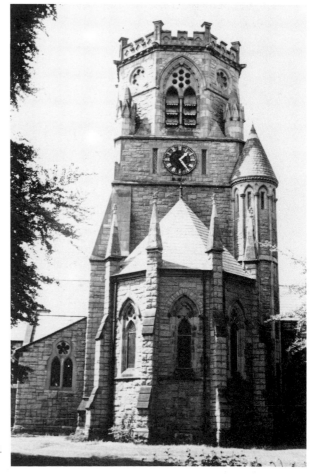

The east end of St Bartholomew's.
PHOTO PETER COSTELLO

Church of the Sacred Heart, Donnybrook

[ROMAN CATHOLIC]

The original eighteenth-century church was close beside the Anglican church (an ancient foundation) in the graveyard in the village of Donnybrook where one wall of it can be seen flanking the police station.

Donnybrook was then infamous for its annual three-day horse fair in August. With the expansion of the city the local residents became disgusted by the scenes of debauchery and had the fair suppressed in 1855. A leading figure in buying out the medieval Royal patent was Fr Nowlan, who worked to have a new church built in reparation for all the past sins with which Donnybrook was associated. He collected funds for the church widely, even soliciting the Empress Eugénie for £1,000.

The intended architect was Patrick Byrne, but after his death the design of Pugin and Ashlin was adopted. (A lithograph of their conception hangs in the church.) Their spire was never built (cost again), and in the 1920s the parish priest of the day had the ornamental parapet added to finish off the stub. The church was dedicated by Cardinal Cullen in 1866.

Among the many attractive features of the church are the stained glass windows (St Patrick, St Eithne and St Feidhlim) by Michael Healy. The fine mosaic work around the high and side altars dates from the 1950s.

St Mary's, Anglesea Road, Donnybrook

[CHURCH OF IRELAND]

St Mary's which replaced an older church of the same name which stood in Donnybrook graveyard, was built at the junction of Anglesea Road and Simmonscourt Road in 1827 (on land that belonged to Christ Church Cathedral) at a recorded cost of £4,143 16s 11d. The communion vessels and registers of the old church were transferred here. So too was the baptismal font in which W.B. Yeats was baptised in 1865.

This church was on a much grander scale altogether than its humble predecessor and was intended to cater for the then rapidly expanding neighbourhood. It was one of the first of the series of gothic churches which was to be the preferred style of the Anglicans in the first part of the century.

The drawing by the archaeologist and topographer George Petrie shows the church as it was soon after dedication. The spire which he shows was damaged in a severe storm on 6 January 1839 and had to be taken down.

Church of the Sacred Heart in the 1880s, before the additions to the tower.
LAWRENCE COLLECTION. NATIONAL LIBRARY OF IRELAND

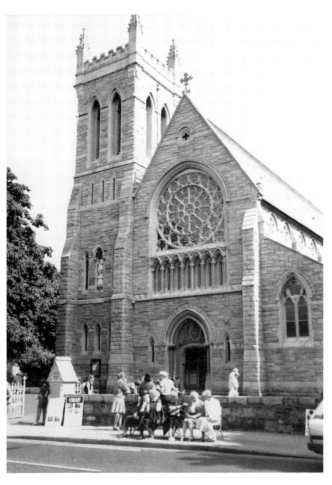

St Mary's, Donnybrook.
PAINTING BY GEORGE PETRIE. NATIONAL GALLERY OF IRELAND

Modern exterior of the Church of the Sacred Heart.
PHOTO PETER COSTELLO

Christ Church, Sandymount

[METHODIST CHURCH/PRESBYTERIAN CHURCH]

Standing just off the Green at Sandymount, this small church now houses a united congregation of Methodists and Presbyterians. It was built by the Methodists, but a union of congregations in the 1970s provided a sensible solution for the 100 people who use the church. The original Methodist style has been altered to accommodate the Presbyterian tradition. This unusual congregation exists in what is also an unusual church, fronted by a large lawn fringed with rose bushes. The low flat façade of granite with a small rose window is found to conceal a nave about four feet narrower. The building is a plain one with simple single lights and no apse. The attractive porch is a memorial addition of 1911.

Sandymount in the early part of the nineteenth century was an isolated seaside resort, which gave itself enough airs to charge 1d for its bathing boxes, driving many of the gentry back to Irishtown which was cheaper. Today it separates the grandeur of Park Avenue from the seediness of Irishtown.

St John the Evangelist, Sandymount

[CHURCH OF IRELAND]

This is one of the most charming churches in Dublin, the work of Thomas Henry Wyatt. Alas it was built of soft Caen stone in imitation of the simple early Norman churches of northern France. Lady Herbert, who took a great interest in the church, was responsible for the use of such an unsuitable stone, which has not lasted in the climate of modern Dublin. The ruthlessly rotted stone-work is sad to see.

This has always been an Anglican church in the Catholic tradition (along with St Bartholomew's, Clyde Road and All Saints, Grangegorman). John Betjeman worshipped here when he lived in Dublin as a British attaché during the war.

The simple early English appeal of the church is enhanced by the detailed carvings, though these too are marred today by decay. The chimney of the vestry, for instance, is wreathed by gargoyle heads and a sinuous dragon. Wyatt was English, and he also worked in Dublin on Sandford Church and St Bartholomew's.

Façade of Christ Church, Sandymount.
PHOTO PETER COSTELLO

St John's, Sandymount.
PHOTO PETER COSTELLO

St Mary's, Church Road, Crumlin

[CHURCH OF IRELAND]

Standing hard by the old eighteenth-century church and its vandalised graveyard, St Mary's comes as a complete surprise. Built in 1942 to the design of Lionel Dixon of McDonnell and Dixon, it is the last Anglican church to be erected in the Dublin area. It is a remarkable piece of work. Modern with art deco metal windows and doors, it is constructed in an attractive burnt-yellow brick. The planes of the outer walls are relieved by triangular buttresses. The bell-tower is squared off, in a chunky modernist way. The interior, too, is equally well designed, with a gothic touch to impart a traditional flavour. The whole building is effective, worthy and well constructed (standing as it does on granite footings). Alas, both the church and the school to the rere have suffered from malicious vandals, and the elements of essential protection added to the church are unfortunate. But it is a church worth going a little out of the way to see, as its highly English style makes it unusual in Ireland at that date.

Our Lady of Dolours, Dolphin's Barn

[ROMAN CATHOLIC]

The church was opened in 1893 as a chapel-of-ease to St James's, and 1902 it was made a parish in its own right. It was well sited near the Grand Canal on the South Circular Road leading north to the Phoenix Park. When it was built this was on the outer edge of a very respectable middle-class area which ran back to Harcourt Street. However, the other road on which it stands runs back through Cork Street into quite the oldest part of the city. As an inner-city area it has since seen much decay, social and material, suffering as so much of the city has from the long-term intentions of the road planners who have spread a blight over the inner areas. The church with its rustic granite masonry and its strong square tower is a fine piece of work. The interior is gently old fashioned and prayerful, with some nice stained glass from the period 1897-1901. The original altar has been moved forward and a new tabernacle erected, blending new with the old.

Side view of St Mary's.
PHOTO PETER COSTELLO

Front façade of St Mary's.
PHOTO PETER COSTELLO

Our Lady's church, Dolphin's Barn.
PHOTO PETER COSTELLO

The Annunciation, Rathfarnham
[ROMAN CATHOLIC]

Standing on a corner site, the church was opened and consecrated in March 1878, though the parish dates back to before the Reformation. The church is not over large, with an attractive gothic façade which includes a statue of the Virgin Mary. The holy-water stoop at the main door is a roughly cut stone trough brought from the old eighteenth-century church. The most unusual feature of the church is the stained glass windows which incorporate the Stations of the Cross. They are the work of Maison Eugene Denis of Nantes and date from the turn of the century when there was great enthusiasm for things Breton in Ireland. The colours are bright and over strong compared with the older glass in the side of the chapel windows. The village was known for the Jesuit house of studies in Rathfarnham Castle, a place of spiritual retreat for several generations of Dublin boys and men. Nearby also is Loreto College, founded in 1822.

St Joseph's, Terenure
[ROMAN CATHOLIC]

The church was designed and built by W.H. Byrne in 1904. A drawing of his first conception hangs just inside the porch. Outside, the building is faced with Wicklow granite, and inside with Aberdeen granite. The railings and gates facing the road were erected in 1916. The fine east window, *The Crucifixion* by Harry Clarke, was erected in 1920. The church has been extended to twice its original size, and now has the altar in the centre of what is a short-armed cruciform plan. On display is a letter to the builder of the church, Canon Terence Anderson, from Pope Pius in 1907 hoping for the speedy erection of the tower. It was never built. The local legend is that under Canon Law while the church is 'unfinished' it need not pay 'Peter's Pence', the annual collection for the Vatican. In the grounds, in an iron cage of its own, hangs the bell (1903) intended for the tower.

Front of Rathfarnham church.
PHOTO PETER COSTELLO

*The caged bell of
St Joseph's in Terenure.*
PHOTO PETER COSTELLO

St Paul of the Cross, Mount Argus, Harold's Cross

[PASSIONIST FATHERS]

The site of the retreat house of the Passionist Fathers was bought in 1856, work began on the monastery in 1859 and it was dedicated in 1863. The first rector was Paul Pakenham, grand-uncle of Lord Longford.

Standing on a small eminence in what was then countryside, Mount Argus made an impressive sight. Indeed, it was the custom of the Passionists to seek remote rural retreats. But in the century and a quarter since, the city has encompassed them.

The monastery was designed by Patrick Byrne according to the rule of the Order, which was influenced by Italian Romanesque models. The course of the work was troubled, the Rector Fr Dominic O'Neill referring in a letter to J.J. McCarthy (the superintendent of the works) to the monastery 'which we cannot by any means regard with satisfaction'. But it is now more highly thought of by the community.

For the church J.J. McCarthy was appointed architect. The church was begun in 1873 and completed in 1878. The Italian Romanesque was out of line with McCarthy's usual gothic preferences. The church consists of a long nave with two side aisles, clerestory windows and a round apse.

On the height of the pediments stands a gold-painted statue of St Michael the Archangel, and in the tympanum below an elaborate depiction of the Passion is carved in high relief.

The church was extended in 1936, and has recently undergone an extensive and expensive restoration, being re-dedicated in October 1986.

It was here that the monumental mason James Pearse (father of Patrick and Willie Pearse) was received into the church. His firm made the pulpit for the church. After 1916 Desmond FitzGerald was hidden in the monastery.

In the popular mind the church is associated with Blessed Charles, a Dutch-born priest who came to Ireland in 1857, and whose work as a confessor and among the poor of Dublin was legendary. It is recorded that up to 300 people a day came to see him, both Catholic and Protestant, from Ireland and abroad. After his death his reputation continued to grow as many favours were linked to his intercession.

He died on 5 January 1893, and having been proclaimed 'a man of heroic virtue' in 1979, he was beatified by Pope John Paul II in 1988. The movement to have him canonised grows every year.

For a century this has been the particular church of the Dublin police, and more lately associated with entertainment and media communities. For many years the Prior, Fr Brian D'Arcy, was himself a well-known journalist. Since 1974 Mount Argus has been a parish church.

Mount Argus, church and monastery wing.
PHOTO WILLIAM STRAFORD

Tomb of Blessed Charles of Mount Argus.
COURTESY FR BRIAN D'ARCY

The façade of the church, showing the elaborate relief of the Passion below the gilded statue of St Michael.
PHOTO ROBERT ALLEN

Methodist Church, Brighton Road, Rathgar

[METHODIST CHURCH IN IRELAND]

On the road leading out of Brighton Square (where Joyce was born in 1882), Rathgar Methodist Church was designed by Thomas Holbrook and erected in 1874. This was then a developing middle-class area, and Brighton Road itself a street with a mixture of house styles and sizes.

In 1924, the jubilee year of its foundation, the church was extended by the erection of transepts as a memorial to the congregation's dead of the Great War: an unusual memorial in Ireland, but perhaps typically Methodist.

This simple gothic church has a short spire, a nave and aisles three bays long. There is a three-light east window. Constructed in a rustic granite, it is charming piece of suburban religious architecture.

Zion Church, Zion Road, Rathgar

[CHURCH OF IRELAND]

Standing on the corner of Bushy Park Road and Zion Road, this church was built in 1861 by Joseph Welland, the architect of the Board of First Fruits, and his partner of the day, Gillespie, at a total cost of over £11,000. He turned to the gothic, and this church is in the Early English style and cruciform in plan. It is built of local black calp, granite and limestone, though inside there are columns of Caen stone. The off-centre tower and spire are the main feature of the church. The north transept was partitioned off in 1984 and discreetly converted into three small office units, the rents from which go some way towards maintaining the church.

Zion began as a Trustee church, established by evangelical members of the Church of Ireland, who espoused a simplicity of worship and a faithfulness to gospel preaching, largely with money from a John Goold. In 1921 the Trustees vested the church in the Representative Body and Zion was made a separate parish.

Brighton Road Methodist Church.
PHOTO PETER COSTELLO

Exterior of Zion Church.
PHOTO PETER COSTELLO

Christt Church, Rathgar

[PRESBYTERIAN CHURCH IN IRELAND]

Completed and opened in 1859, this church is a match to the Abbey church on the north side. It was again the work of the Scottish architect, Andrew Heiton, who used a rustic granite masonry.

This was an important site, facing as it does the village of Rathgar. It was one of the sites selected for Zion Church originally. The front façade of the church stands on a small eminence, but slopes away to the rere, allowing for a basement church hall very like that in the York Road church. It has a nave, lit by 3 two-light windows with plain glass with shallow two-bay transepts and a square chancel. The tower is elegant in its proportions. In the grounds are a sexton's house built with the church and a modern extension which is practical rather than attractive.

The church body is an active one, drawing members from all over the south side, but the neighbourhood, though once again on the rise, for a long time contained few of the prosperous businessmen and their families for whom the church was erected.

The Three Patrons, Rathgar Road

[ROMAN CATHOLIC]

The foundation stone of the Church of the Three Patrons was laid in 1881. Rathgar, a district of wide wealthy tree-lined streets, became a separate parish from Rathmines when it was dedicated the following year. The 'three patrons' are saints Patrick, Brigid and Columcille.

The façade by W.H. Byrne was erected in 1891, for the sides and rere of the church are plainer, with blind windows. There was to have been a pillared portico in addition but this was never erected.

Statues of the three patrons rise above the high altar. There is an ambulatory around the nave and chancel, an unusual feature in a Catholic church (but also found in the Pro-Cathedral). The paintings of the Stations in the aisles and the mysteries of the Rosary in the nave are also unusual and very fine. The interior is more Roman in flavour, contrasting with the classical façade.

Christ Church, Rathgar about 1910.
AUTHOR'S COLLECTION

Christ Church today.
PHOTO PETER COSTELLO

The Three Patrons, just before the Great War.
AUTHOR'S COLLECTION

Mary Immaculate Refuge of Sinners, Rathmines

[ROMAN CATHOLIC]

During the nineteenth century Rathmines was a separate township with its own town hall and local government. For other Dubliners it had a rather snobbish reputation (reflected by Sean O'Casey, with his jokes about the local accent in *The Plough and the Stars*). But in fact it was a very mixed area which included all classes and creeds. The housing was however nearly all newly built and so of a higher quality than in the inner city.

The parish of Rathmines was created from St Nicholas-Without in 1823. But Mass was said in the parish priest, Canon Stafford's house in Portobello Place, in Milltown at the chapel there or in Harold's Cross.

In 1830 on the present site a small chapel was erected on land purchased from the Earl of Meath. Gothic in style it was opened by Dr Murray in August 1830. But the area was expanding, this small church was soon outgrown and by mid-century a new one was needed.

So the present church was built in 1854. It was designed 'in the Greek style' by Patrick Byrne, and later extended by W.H. Byrne, who added the portico and pediment inscribed *Mariae Immaculatae Refugio Pecatorum*, on which stand the statues of The Virgin, St Peter (or St Celestine) and St Patrick by Patrick Farrell.

Nicknamed Canon Fricker's church, it was adorned with many paintings and decorations. A fire destroyed the church in January 1920, but it was rebuilt and reopened on 4 July 1922, at which time the copper dome was enlarged, creating the famous landmark on the south city. But the debt and the work were not out of the way until after 1932.

The Dogma of the Immaculate Conception had been proclaimed in 1854, and the dedication seemed most appropriate to Cardinal Cullen when he opened the church in 1856.

The great houses that run away on each side were single family homes, as were the houses towards Rathgar and Milltown. But Rathmines lost its independence under the Free State, and the township went into decline from which parts of it around the church have never recovered. From the 1920s on, this has been an area of digs and flats, and it is this transitory population that forms the congregation today. It is for this largely young population that a modern folk Mass is provided each Sunday evening.

The front façade of the church.
PHOTO PETER COSTELLO

The rere view of Rathmines church.
PHOTO PETER COSTELLO

Grosvenor Baptist Church, Rathmines

[BAPTIST UNION IN IRELAND]

The two main Baptist churches in Dublin, at Phibsborough and Rathmines, are both attractive buildings, of which the Rathmines one is perhaps the best known as well as the most interesting. (There is also a small chapel in Pearse Street.)

Standing on a corner site in a quiet neighbourhood of the city it presents a mid-gothic aspect to the world. The essence of the Baptist creed is the saving commitment of adult baptism, and in 1989 the east end of the church was rebuilt and fitted with a pool for plunging candidates. The Baptist Church has an immense following in America, but in these islands its extent has always been limited. The Baptists are marked by their enthusiasm and the pride of place assigned to hymn singing.

This church, however, belongs solidly in the mid-Victorian tradition of church building. It was built in the 1870s by English Baptists. For a period it was used as a hall by the Plymouth Brethren, the Baptists returning again in 1942. It has an interesting arrangement of arches at the main entrance and an attractive towered façade, but inside is quite plain, being simply painted in green, with no decoration. A flat ceiling has been installed instead of the original vaulted one, which is a slight loss.

Holy Trinity, Church Avenue, Rathmines

[CHURCH OF IRELAND]

Another of the Dublin churches of John Semple, 'the presiding genius of the Board of First Fruits' in Maurice Craig's phrase. It has his distinctive pinnacles and deep-set windows and doors. The three wide gables, the tall steeple, and the rather plain exterior are all typical of the period and the architect.

The church was opened in September 1833, and stands on an island in the middle of the road where Belgrave Road meets Church Avenue. It was erected at a time when the upper parts of Rathmines Road and Palmerstown Road were being developed. Rathmines was a separate township, in which much of the actual wealth of Dublin was then located, as the broad roads and large houses indicate.

144

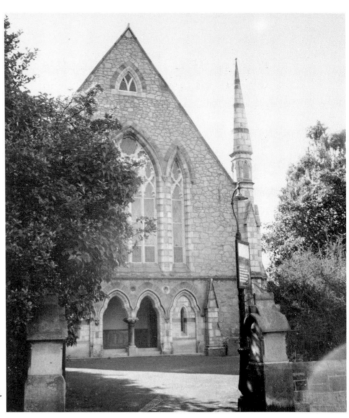

Grosvenor Road Baptist Church.
PHOTO PETER COSTELLO

Holy Trinity in Rathmines.
PHOTO PETER COSTELLO

Holy Name, Beechwood Avenue

[ROMAN CATHOLIC]

As the houses around it indicate, the church belongs to the turn of the century. A wooden chapel-of-ease was the first church on the site, erected in 1897. A Mr Scully donated a plot of land and No. 21 Beechwood Avenue to the parish. Two other donations of £6,000 and £10,000 followed from others. The church itself was begun in 1907, a year after Cullenswood was made a separate parish from Rathgar.

The neighbourhood was in a sense an isolated one, cut off behind the main Sandford Road and the railway line, but it was nevertheless a popular place of residence, used by Joyce in his play *Exiles* to epitomise a certain kind of respectable Dublin. Yet down to 1830 wildfowl were shot in winter over the fields here. But the arrival of the railway line to Wicklow altered all of that.

The church is finely built, the tower combining a round belfry in a very striking manner. The interior of the church is notable for a mosaic of the symbols of the Evangelists in the sanctuary.

Assumption of the Blessed Virgin, Milltown

[ROMAN CATHOLIC]

Often overlooked in its situation, this church is among the most interesting in the area. Under the dedication of St Gall and St Columbanus it was a chapel-of-ease to Donnybrook, only becoming a parish church in 1974, even though it dates back to Georgian times. It is said that it was originally a barn used for Mass in penal times, which escaped destruction by Cromwellian troops because they did not realise what it was used for. The house was rebuilt by the Franciscans in 1819, with some small changes later in the century. It was extended, refronted and for some odd reason rededicated in 1935, but inside it retains a very attractive old-fashioned air, enhanced by paintings and plaques from the earlier period.

Milltown was once a pleasure resort of Dubliners who frequented a shebeen that stood on the Dodder bank beside the old bridge (dating back to the sixteenth century) which carried the road to Dundrum.

The Holy Name, about 1932.
AUTHOR'S COLLECTION

A holy-water font in the Assumption dedicated to the memory of Patrick Doyle, a 1916 insurrectionary.
PHOTO PETER COSTELLO

St Gall and St Columbanus, now the Assumption.
PHOTO PETER COSTELLO

St Philip's, Milltown

[CHURCH OF IRELAND]

In contrast to the local Catholic church, this Anglican church stands among the houses of a mid-Victorian development around Palmerston Park (named for the British Prime Minister who died in 1865) of which it is the centrepiece.

Milltown was the property from the eighteenth century on of the Leeson family, afterwards the Lords Milltown. There was then only a small chapel-of-ease (to St Peter's) which served the needs of the growing number of worshippers. In 1857 Milltown was made a separate parish and the present church was erected. The architect was Sir Thomas Drew and the builder William Doolin of Westland Row. The church was consecrated on the Feast of St Philip and St James (1 May) in 1867.

Though it is by no means a large church, Drew's sense of design gives the nave and sanctuary an air of spaciousness. The entrance is an unusual 'cloister porch' which served not only as a pleasing feature to the church but also (as the *Ecclesiastical Gazette* observed at the time) 'to give shelter to a slowly leaving congregation in inclement weather'. Many of the streets in the neighbourhood of Palmerston Park are very well-preserved examples of fine 1870s architecture.

Sandford Church, Ranelagh

[CHURCH OF IRELAND]

Sandford Church was originally a small chapel-of-ease to St Peter's, erected by Robert Newenham who lived in Merton House and who got George Baron Mountsandford to provide the site and money for an evangelical chapel and school. Opened on 26 June 1826, it was a plain building in granite rubble, flanked by two cottages. In 1858 Sandford became a parish, and in 1860 the façade was rebuilt in granite masonry with a carved memorial porch to Archdeacon William Irwin, designed by Lanyon, Lynn and Lanyon of Belfast.

In 1880 the side aisles and chancel apse were added. Recent redecoration has removed the old evangelical texts from the chancel arch, but a remarkable Harry Clarke creation (two lights depicting St Peter and St Paul with the scene of the Road to Damascus and the Denial of Our Lord) from 1921 is among a set of fine windows. The church gave its name to the road to Milltown, which built up from 1860 to 1900.

St Philip's at Palmerston Park.
PHOTO PETER COSTELLO

Harry Clarke window (1921) in Sandford Church.
PHOTO PETER COSTELLO

Sandford Church in Ranelagh.
PHOTO PETER COSTELLO

Our Lady Queen of Peace, Merrion Road

[ROMAN CATHOLIC]

Built in the Romanesque style much favoured by Catholic parishes during the interwar period, this church was opened in 1954. The distinctive copper clad roof was then an unusual feature. So too was the copper-domed round tower which echoes rather than imitates the ancient form of Irish round tower. The use of a fence breaks the vast amount of space that has to be devoted to car parking, making the church more intimate. The interior, in contrast, is quite plain. Recently the roof has had to be extensively repaired, leaving it an odd pattern of oxidised and raw copper panels.

Our Lady Star of the Sea, Sandymount

[ROMAN CATHOLIC]

One of the more interesting churches of its period, the foundation stone of Star of the Sea was laid in May 1851, creating a new parish out of what had been part of Donnybrook and Irishtown.

The granite church, designed by J.J. McCarthy, then stood on the seashore, and the three almost equal gables give it an unusual appearance. During the course of construction a severe storm blew down a front gable end, some of the stone-work and part of the roof frame. Despite this setback, it was finally completed in 1858. A tower was never built, but additions were made in 1889-91.

The windows in the west end have a more elaborate decorated appearance. The stained glass is attractive, especially some pieces from the turn of the century. Statues of St Joseph, St Patrick and The Blessed Virgin are set into the exterior walls. Some insensitive changes and additions have been made in recent years to the back.

Joyce features the church in *Ulysses*, taking care to write home to his aunt to inquire what the trees in Leahy's Terrace were and whether there were steps down to the beach. There were, but a roadway driven through in the 1920s has altered the whole lie of the land. Yet 'the quiet church whence there streamed forth at times upon the stillness the voice of prayer to her who is in her pure radiance a beacon ever to the storm tossed heart of man, Mary, star of the sea,' was nevertheless invoked in imaginative detail down to the supper of chops with catsup consumed by the parish clergy.

Exterior of Merrion Road church.
PHOTO PETER COSTELLO

Front façade of Star of the Sea.
PHOTO PETER COSTELLO

St Teresa of the Child Jesus, Donore Avenue

[ROMAN CATHOLIC]

Though the parish was only created from the ancient parish of St Catherine in 1946, the church was built in the 1920s as one of several to cope with a sudden expansion of the city to the west which coincided with the elevation of Archbishop Byrne in 1921. The exterior with its simple gable and two side aisles is attractively uncomplicated. The grounds were originally well laid out, 'parked' as a contemporary writer observed. In front of the church is a statue of St Teresa, the Little Flower, and also a Lourdes grotto erected by the parishioners themselves. The devotion to St Teresa, who died in 1582, was first cultivated in St Catherine's parish.

The church backs on to Fatima Mansions, which have a certain notoriety. A local character remarked to me that things were so bad that the parish priest had to have security guards at the Sunday Masses to prevent handbags being stolen.

St Catherine and St James's, Donore Avenue

[CHURCH OF IRELAND]

Originally dedicated to St Victor, this church was built in 1896 as a chapel-of-ease for St Catherine's parish. It then consisted only of the nave and sat 250, but was packed to the doors for two services on Sunday. Between 1911 and 1914 the chancel, transepts and tower were added. The dedication was to provide a link with the Augustinian Canons of St Victor who lived in St Thomas's Abbey.

In 1969 it was given its present dedication, on the closure of the old inner-city churches, which are described below. Those churches have been an essential part of the life of Dublin; the present church belongs to the new life of the suburbs, where the future of the Anglican community lies with families rearing young children.

St Teresa's church in Donore Avenue.
PHOTO PETER COSTELLO

The former St Victor's in Donore Avenue.
PHOTO PETER COSTELLO

The Royal Hospital, Kilmainham

The Royal Hospital after years of sad neglect has emerged like some wonderful butterfly to a new and important role in the cultural life of the city.

The institution here dates back to the time of Strongbow, who granted the lands at Kilmainham to the Knights of St John for a charity hospital. At the Reformation the lands passed into the hands of the Crown. In 1680 Charles II created a new hospital or home for old soldiers on the site, along the lines of Chelsea Hospital in London.

The design is based on Les Invalides in Paris. The architect was William Robinson, the King's Surveyor-General in Ireland. He is the first Irish 'architect' about whom anything is known.

The main part of the buildings was finished in 1684, though the chapel itself, the central part of the plan, was not finished till 1687. With a tower added in 1701, the cost was £24,000. It is, as Maurice Craig observes, the oldest surviving secular building in the country.

The chapel, which was off the main dining room, is a magnificent piece of work. It was dedicated to Charles I 'King and Martyr', in his role as an Anglican saint. The wood panelling and carving, especially rich at the east end, were the work of Huguenot craftsman James Tabary, and have been restored to perfection.

The ceiling today is actually of papier mâché, for the old ceiling had to be taken down in 1902, though the replica very accurately reflects the quality of the original stucco work. A riot of fruits and foliage restrained within frames of plainer work, it is the real glory of the hospital, the creation of an unknown artist of great genius. Into the high east window which faces towards the city stone and glass from the old priory were reworked. The cast iron gates which close the chapel date from the reign of Queen Anne.

The hospital was used for army pensioners, Irish men of course, until the advent of the Free State. In 1927 the surviving pensioners were moved to Chelsea, and the last service held in the chapel. Until 1949 it was used by the Civic Guards. It then passed into the hands of the National Museum as a store. In 1985 after complete restoration it was reopened for concerts, exhibitions and lectures.

Though the chapel is no longer used for religious services, it is still availed of for recitals of chamber music, in a way an appropriate reflection of the spiritual purpose for which it was created. After long decades of shabby neglect, visitors can once again appreciate what is without doubt one of the finest places of worship in the city.

Interior of the chapel.
COURTESY ROYAL HOSPITAL, KILMAINHAM

Mary Immaculate, Tyrconnell Road, Inchicore

[OBLATE FATHERS]

Built in the 1870s, this impressive chapel attached to the Oblate retreat house was completed only in the 1920s with the addition of the bell-towers. One of these contains a carillon in the Continental style, which plays tunes rather than changes. It was arranged to be able to play 'The Bells of the Angelus' on each hour. A lavishly appointed church, the most interesting feature is a stained glass window *The Calling of the Apostles*, an unusual subject.

From an early date there was a devotion to Our Lady of Lourdes here, which eventually led to the erection of 'the Irish Lourdes' in the grounds to the rere of the church in 1930. In two years it was estimated that a million people had visited the shrine, which was the inspiration of many similar shrines at churches all over the country. Also, a huge crib is a feature of the grounds at Christmastime, with wax figures and shepherds' clothes brought specially from Bethlehem. In a reliquary was set a splinter from the Manger (enshrined in the Roman church of St Mary Major since the twelfth century). The copy of the statue of St Peter in the Vatican commemorated the Diocesan pilgrimage to Rome in 1893.

Congregational Church, Kilmainham

[CONGREGATIONAL UNION IN IRELAND]

Historically the Congregationalists are descended from the Independents of the sixteenth and seventeenth century of whom Oliver Cromwell was one. So too were the Pilgrim Fathers who founded the Bay Colony in the *Mayflower*. They asserted the purely spiritual nature of the faith, and rejected all hierarchies and doctrines that restricted it. They were stern puritans in their personal lives.

Here in Dublin they had arisen in about 1640, and have remained a part of the Protestant community since, though always as a small group. In the last century they had other chapels around the city, but now are reduced to this one curious little chapel at Kilmainham, its stark plainness relieved by period gothic sash windows. It was built as the Salem Chapel in 1814 by Obadiah Willan, a Yorkshire mill owner, along with the cottages opposite for the workers in his mill on the Camac. There are now only about thirty members of the congregation.

Children kissing the toe of St Peter.
PHOTO PETER COSTELLO

The Oblate Fathers' church at Inchicore.
PHOTO PETER COSTELLO

The Congregational Church in Kilmainham.
PHOTO PETER COSTELLO

The Nativity, Chapelizod

[ROMAN CATHOLIC]

Part of the ancient parish of Clondalkin until 1955, the Nativity is a relatively new church, dating only from the mid-nineteenth century, for a very old village. Standing on the road into Chapelizod from Dublin, it is an imposing sight though it must have been over-large for the needs of the parish when built.

Chapelizod is named for Isolde, the daughter of King Mark of Dublin in the Arthurian tales and Wagnerian opera, of whom Tristan is enamoured. But there is nothing over-coloured or extravagant about the period charm of the present church. Until 1972 the parish included Palmerstown on the other side of the river. The essential alterations for the new liturgy have been done with a simplicity that reflects the undecorated gothic nature of the church.

Devotees of Joyce will know that not only was his father secretary of the distillery here, but his Mr Duffy in the *Dubliners (A Painful Case)* lived here from preference 'because he found all the other suburbs of Dublin mean, modern and pretentious'.

St Laurence's, Chapelizod

[CHURCH OF IRELAND]

Built in 1832, in a gothic style that was then popular as a rural alternative to the classical urbanities of such churches as St Georges's, this is the church made famous in Sheridan Le Fanu's novel, *The House by the Churchyard*, which features not only the churchyard in the village, but a sensitive young Anglican clergyman and a rumbustious Catholic priest, all drawn from the village life of Chapelizod as he observed it in his youth during the 1820s. The house itself still stands in the village, by the lane that leads to the church. The tower of the church dates from the fourteenth century, but was remodelled in 1859. The interior is now quite plain, aside from memorial tablets.

The Nativity in Chapelizod.
PHOTO PETER COSTELLO

Interior of The Nativity.
PHOTO PETER COSTELLO

The interior of St Laurence's today.
PHOTO PETER COSTELLO

St Laurence's in Chapelizod.
PHOTO PETER COSTELLO

The Assumption, Booterstown

[ROMAN CATHOLIC]

This church was for a long time the parish church of a wide area of what was then rural Dublin. Inside the church can be found a tablet recording the names of the parish priests from 1616 on.

The church itself, however, belongs to the early nineteenth century. The land on which it was built was given by Mrs Barbara Verschoyle (commemorated by another tablet) who aroused the interest in it of the landlord of the immediate district, Lord Fitzwilliam, 'her attached friend and patron'. There is also a memorial to members of the Madden family who lived in the parish, Dr Madden being the well-known historian of the United Irishmen.

The church has been enlarged and improved, and the school buildings that face the main road are all nineteenth century. The handcarved Stations are in pleasing contrast with the Georgian decor such as the Lamb and Flag over the altar. Behind the church is the presbytery, an attractive Georgian house. The church does not face the road, and as required by the penal regulations does not immediately suggest a church, having domestic rather than ecclesiastical windows. It is among the most interesting of early Catholic churches in Dublin and worthy of a visit.

Booterstown, which then had a fine beach, was a popular summer resort in late Georgian times, but the coming of the railway which created the slob lands (now a bird reserve) between the embankment and the shore ruined all that. Today aside from being a pleasant suburb it is noted for its schools, the Catholic Blackrock College and the Protestant St Andrew's.

The main entrance, showing the Georgian façade.
PHOTO PETER COSTELLO

The northern aspect of Booterstown church.
PHOTO PETER COSTELLO

St Philip and St James, Booterstown

[CHURCH OF IRELAND]

Booterstown parish was founded in May 1821, from the much extended parish of St Mary's, Donnybrook. The city, in the form of large detached houses, has spread out into the county. Two men were responsible for creating the parish, the 11th Earl of Pembroke, the landlord who gave the ground, and the banker James Digges La Touche. Lord Pembroke also provided £1,000 towards the cost of the church. The names of Joseph Welland, who was supervising architect for the Church authorities, and John Bowden have been connected with the design and building of the church. The parapets and pinnacles are very typical of Irish Anglican churches of the period. The cost was £4,615 7s 8¼d — an exact account if ever there was. The church was consecrated on 16 May 1824.

Over the decades after the coming of the railway, larger houses were joined by developments of middle-class housing, and in 1867 it was decided to enlarge the building by adding a chancel and a south transept. In 1876 a north transept and organ chamber were built, leaving the church much as it stands today. Among later decorations the striking mosaic of *Christ Blessing the Children* was commissioned as a memorial to his wife by Henry Dowse in the 1960s.

Among the personalities connected with the parish there stands out Field Marshall Lord Gough, one of the most prominent generals of his time, and the novelist Nevil Shute who lived for a long time in Booterstown with his family. De Valera lived for much of his life in Cross Avenue, and in August 1927 Kevin O'Higgins was assassinated outside Sans Soucie — a small cross in the pavement marks the site. This brutal act was out of character with what is essentially a quiet neighbourhood.

The church from Cross Avenue.
PHOTO PETER COSTELLO

The main body of the church from the south.
PHOTO PETER COSTELLO

All Saints, Blackrock

[CHURCH OF IRELAND]

Set in a fine road built up between 1840 and 1880, All Saints is itself a very attractive church with unusual features. It consists of a nave, side aisles and a square tower with a short spire. There is a square apse and transept.

The main windows of the nave are triangular in shape — an unusual feature found also in Christ Church, Park Road, further south in Dun Laoghaire. It is lit largely from clerestory windows. The church and the rectory to the rere are both built in rustic granite. The buildings face on to Proby Square, an unusual creation in its own right where the historian and genealogist Edward MacLysaght had a garden centre during the years he lived there.

All Saints is now united with Stillorgan, a common practice in the Church of Ireland to create a functional parish. Services are still offered in both churches, however.

St John the Baptist, Blackrock

[ROMAN CATHOLIC]

This impressive church was designed by Patrick Byrne in 1842. It was built on a site donated by Lord Cloncurry — whose villa was at Maretimo — and dedicated in 1845. A tablet on the tower, now partly obscured, records it was erected in gratitude for the gift of temperance, those being the days of Fr Mathew's crusades against drink. Additions in a plainer style were made in 1850 and 1856, and most recently an extension has been put on to the west end. The interior is lofty and decorated with period vaultings. There is a elaborate gothic reredos of the Apostles and a gothic pulpit. Over the door is an entablature of John baptising Christ in the Jordan. There are windows by the Early Studios of Camden Street, who provided glass to a great many Dublin churches around the turn of the century, and more modern artistic work by Evie Hone and Harry Clarke.

When the church was built Blackrock was a quieter place than it is today. Joyce, who lived here in 1892, describes a visit to the church and how he wondered what his uncle was praying for: 'Perhaps he prayed for the souls in purgatory or for the grace of a happy death or perhaps he prayed that God might send him back a part of the big fortune he had squandered in Cork.'

All Saints, Blackrock.
PHOTO PETER COSTELLO

New porch with plaque of John the Baptist baptising Christ.
PHOTO PETER COSTELLO

Exterior of John the Baptist church.
PHOTO PETER COSTELLO

Monkstown Church, Monkstown

[CHURCH OF IRELAND]

This wonderful creation of John Semple, lord of creation at the Board of First Fruits, is a church about which there have always been mixed feelings, for it has been both loved and loathed. The old church, which had been a simple preaching box dating from 1789, was taken down and replaced by 1833 with what one writer refers to as 'the nondescript edifice which now disfigures the site'. Gothic in intention it has also Moorish elements, inspired perhaps by the Alhambra in Granada. (Washington Irving's *Tales of the Alhambra* had appeared in 1832.)

All Semple's churches are distinctive. This church is very impressive as it is approached from the Dublin road, and fills its site to good effect. John Betjeman was enchanted by it, as who would not be. But it must strike many as being too unusual to be a church, with an almost irreligious restlessness about it. Semple had provided the interior with galleries in the transepts and a very Protestant arrangement at the east end which emphasised the pulpit. Too Protestant perhaps, for by the 1860s it had been changed to more Catholic liturgical arrangements which do not fit with his starker notions. His work according to Betjeman, 'now seems bold, modern, vast and original'.

St Patrick's, Monkstown

[ROMAN CATHOLIC]

In complete contrast to the bravura extravagance of Semple's neighbouring Anglican church, St Patrick's stands across the road in an uneasy relationship.

Designed by George Ashlin and the younger Pugin, this exercise in mid-Victorian gothic was erected by 1864. There is some fine carving over the main door, with a statue of the patron saint and scenes from his mission in Ireland. The interior has been repainted largely in a cool lime green with a terracotta roof. The original detailing, even down to the confessionals, has been retained. Nor has the church suffered unkind additions.

At the top of Carrickbrennan Road there is an old graveyard, reached through an arched gateway. This is thought to have been the site of an old Celtic monastery, a predecessor to the medieval Cistercians that give their name to Monkstown. But an investigation in 1885 by archaeologists failed to find any traces of an ancient settlement. In Pakenham Road is a Friends Meeting House of long standing.

Monkstown Church from the Dublin road.
PHOTO PETER COSTELLO

The east façade of Monkstown Church.
PHOTO PETER COSTELLO

St Patrick's in Carrickbrennan Road.
PHOTO PETER COSTELLO

Christ Church, Park Road, Dun Laoghaire

[CHURCH OF IRELAND]

Originally called Dun Leary, the title of Kingstown was granted by King William when he departed from here in 1821. This marked the new opening of the packet station in the harbour, which transformed what had been a little fishing village into a port and popular resort, a process completed by 1860.

The Mariner's Church (now the National Maritime Museum) in Haigh Terrace was built in 1837 and extended in 1867, with the intention of serving the sailors who used the port. It is a magnificent church, the features of which have not been obscured by its present use. The three-light east window was erected with the tower in 1865. Christ Church, however, began as an independent bethel and was doubled in size when it became a parish church. Though it retains its original simplicity, it has some nice features. L.A.G. Strong the novelist, who worshipped here as a child, thought that the window of Christ walking on the waves showed trampling on snakes. It commemorates William Cowl, drowned off Zanzibar in 1891. Another memorial is to a parishioner who died of fever in Sierra Leone in 1890. The church was extended in 1879 and then enlarged and beautified in 1887. St Columba's Chapel (which preserves the title of the Mariner's Church) was dedicated in 1975.

St Michael's, Dun Laoghaire

[ROMAN CATHOLIC]

The original church was built in 1894 to the design of C. J. McCarthy. This was a straightforward exercise in gothic, of which only the tower survives, for the church was destroyed by a fire in 1968.

Rather than rebuild the old church, it was decided to replace it by a church in a completely modern idiom. Designed by Pearse McKenna, Naois O'Dowd and Sean Rothery, the new St Michael's was completed by 1973. This has been seen as a landmark church, and has been much admired. It was among the first truly modern churches in the Dublin area and the shock of the new troubled many.

The architectural details are best appreciated, oddly enough, when the church is not in use.

Exterior of Christ Church in Park Road.
PHOTO PETER COSTELLO

ST. MICHAEL'S R.C. CHURCH DUNLAOGHAIRE, CO. DUBLIN

The same view of St Michael's, with the old tower incorporated into the new fabric.
PHOTO PETER COSTELLO

The old St Michael's.
AUTHOR'S COLLECTION

Presbyterian Church, York Road

[PRESBYTERIAN CHURCH IN IRELAND]

This fine church with its neighbouring manse was designed by Andrew Heiton who was also responsible for the Abbey Church in Parnell Square (1864), and for Christ Church in Rathgar (1859). He was a Scot from Perth and (I suppose) a staunch Presbyterian himself, connected with the well-known Dublin coal importers. It was businesses of that kind that paid for these churches. Like Rathgar church, York Road also has its hall in the basement, for the land here slopes back making this unusual arrangement possible. Built in the 1860s, like the other churches it marks an unusual amount of building by the Presbyterians in a short period. The railway had transformed Kingstown, as it then was, and made it possible for many of the wealthy in Dublin to move further out, away from what was already a city in decay. Dublin had ceased to build. All the new building was in suburban streets like York Road.

St John the Evangelist, Mounttown

[SOCIETY OF PIUS X]

Built in the 1860s as one of a series of Anglican churches in the area, St John's was in use as a Protestant church until the 1970s. It was then bought by the Society of Pius X, the followers of Archbishop Lefevre, who espouse the traditional Tridentine Latin Rite. It is now used by a congregation of about 200, but is worth a visit from anyone who wished to see what an Irish Catholic church of the best kind would have looked like over a century ago.

The church was of the plainest kind of simple gothic. The main altar comes from Eccles Street convent and is a fine piece of carving. The side altar comes from the Jesuit house at Rathfarnham Castle. A fine set of Stations (about 1860) came from a country church. There are also several Victorian paintings, including *The Transfiguration*, an unusual subject, which were bought at sales around the country from priests intent on modernising their churches.

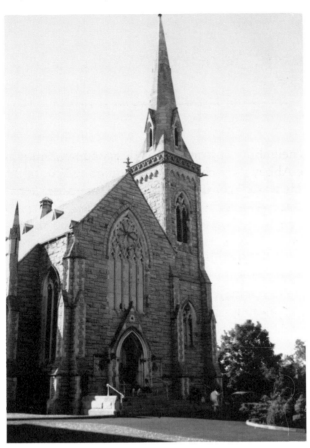

*York Road Presbyterian Church
with young ballet dancers.*
PHOTO PETER COSTELLO

St John the Evangelist in Mounttown
PHOTO PETER COSTELLO

St Paul's Glenageary

[CHURCH OF IRELAND]

A lovely gothic church built in 1868, in rough rustic granite with limestone dressings. The main feature is a square tower with a tall spire and four pinnacles. There is a four-light west window. The body of the church consists of a nave and apse with no side aisles.

The memorials include one to Frances Alice Leonard 'lost in a collison on the Niger River' in 1924. The chancel was enlarged in 1913, and the wooden panels fitted. There is a fine window of the women at the tomb, which is an unusual subject. The walls are plainly painted, making the exterior more interesting.

The church stands at the head of Silchester Road, which developed in the 1870s and is serviced by the nearby railway station. This is an area with many attractive roads, especially Marlborough Road, all of which date from mid-Victorian times.

Our Lady of Victories, Sallynoggin

[ROMAN CATHOLIC]

Though it was only made a separate parish in 1966, Sallynoggin had a church for a decade before that. Built on the high ground behind Glasthule, Our Lady of Victories is a modern church in the middle of Corporation housing development, flanked by the small industrial complex that gives (or rather gave) employment to many of the local residents. It looks out over a bleak enough city landscape.

The church itself has walls of plain rendering, and is Romanesque in style with a classical portico and campanile, which add a discordant note to the building. The colours inside, purple, red and blue, are harsh and discordant too, and the church shows signs of neglect.

Yet the details of the building (even down to such things as the door handles) are very good, as are the wooden fittings of the period. There are handcarved Stations, but these sit uneasily with repository-type statues.

View of the chancel and tower of St Paul's.
PHOTO PETER COSTELLO

Sallynoggin Catholic church.
PHOTO PETER COSTELLO

St Matthias, Ballybrack

[CHURCH OF IRELAND]

St Matthias at Ballybrack is a country church dating from the 1840s which the spread of the city has caught up in its toils: a dual carriageway now begins outside its gates.

This has the deep-set narrow doors and windows and also the pinnacles familiar in the work of John Semple, though this is not by him, but another architect for the Board of First Fruits.

Cruciform in plan, it has a nave with transepts and squared-off chancel, with a bell-tower at the west end. Three-light lancet windows are in the east. The windows have been filled with late Victorian stained glass.

It is typical of many churches which the Board built with great enthusiasm in the early part of the last century. The intention was to reinforce the presence of the Church of Ireland by repairing old churches or providing new ones. The enthusiasm got out of hand in the north of Dublin where a church was built in a parish with no Church of Ireland member, was rarely used, and had to be demolished after seventy years.

It is this rash of churches that the Church of Ireland is now in retreat from, retrenching to a very limited number that can be managed today. But the fate of these country churches remains to be solved. Not all are as well advantaged as St Matthias.

Holy Trinity, Killiney

[CHURCH OF IRELAND]

The arrival of the railway to Bray along the sea coast at Killiney led to the development of the hills behind the coast. Here towards the end of the century a host of houses in their own grounds, behind intimidating stone walls, was built. In the middle of these in Killiney Hill Road, stands Holy Trinity Church, erected in 1858. Tucked in under the slope of the hill, behind its own enclosing wall with only a small area of land, this is an attractive church with short tower topped by a curiously oriental copper cap.

St Matthias in Ballybrack.
PHOTO PETER COSTELLO

Holy Trinity church on Killiney Hill.
PHOTO PETER COSTELLO

St Patrick's, Dalkey
[CHURCH OF IRELAND]

One of the series of Anglican and Catholic churches built out into the south county during the last century, St Patrick's perches on the edge of a quarry from which stone for the local harbour was cut.

Erected in 1843, just three years after the local Catholic church, it is distinguished by the square tower with long narrow openings. The church itself, though it stands on a rise, is also rather squat, cruciform in plan, with three lancet windows in the transepts. The square apse has a large east window in which is set unusual Star of David tracery.

The Church of the Assumption, Dalkey
[ROMAN CATHOLIC]

Situated in the village main street, Dalkey's Catholic church is very near an earlier church, which can be visited. The church was built in 1840, but has been renovated since with the addition of the bell-tower.

The exterior of the church is plain enough, but inside it has simple but attractive fan vaulting and other period features, with shallow transepts and gothic altars. There is a large painting of John the Baptist baptising Christ in the Jordan hanging on the north-west wall.

The unmodernised appearance of the church is particularly attractive, for the Assumption is a model of the kind of church common enough in rural Ireland until recently.

Dalkey too by the peculiar nature of its location, has much of the atmosphere of a country village rather than a suburb. The writer Hugh Leonard in his accounts of his childhood gives a vivid impression of the religious and emotional lives of the people who worship here.

But even now new churches are being built in Killiney and Ballybrack, threatening that special peace of Dalkey. This was the original parish church for the area from Ballybrack to Glasthule. The Catholic church at Ballybrack, an almost Protestant erection of the 1860s, and the more decorated church of Glasthule dating from 1890s, were originally chapels-of-ease.

St Patrick's parish church in Dalkey.
PHOTO PETER COSTELLO

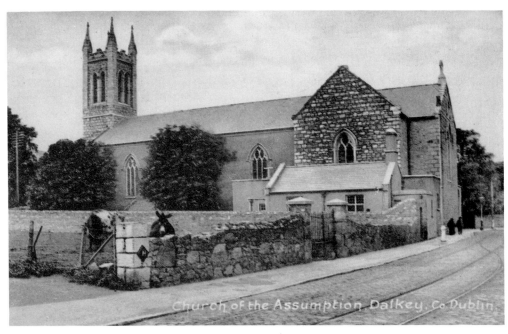

The Church of the Assumption about 1905, in more rural days.
AUTHOR'S COLLECTION

St Therese's, Mount Merrion

[ROMAN CATHOLIC]

M̲ount Merrion takes its name from the Irish residence of the Earl of Pembroke, for all this land around the road to Stillorgan was part of the Pembroke estate. It remained largely rural until the 1940s when the new housing estates, of a largely middle-class nature, were laid out on the slopes to the right of the old road.

In the middle of these St Therese's looms up in that open parking space that bleakly surrounds so many Catholic churches to their disadvantage. The parish was created from Dundrum in 1948. The style of the church is the derived Romanesque so common in Dublin during the episcopate of Dr McQuaid. Built in a finished granite masonry, a pillared façade with the rose window fronts a nave with narrow lancet windows. The transepts too are lit by large rose windows. The square bell-tower built out from the south transept is finished with cupola and pinnacles which provide a touch of panache to an otherwise sober church.

St Thomas's, Foster Avenue

[CHURCH OF IRELAND]

On the corner where Foster Avenue debouches from Mount Merrion into the Stillorgan Road, St Thomas's is a new church for the Anglican community, built in the 1930s to cover the new developments between Booterstown and Dundrum. It is small, neat church of simple design with an unostentatious interior.

The great name associated with it is the Rev. Monk Gibbon, the father of the poet and writer Monk Gibbon, who developed the parish and whose name is attached to the church hall. These names are a reminder that many Anglicans were like the father deeply concerned with the treasures of Ireland's past, or like the son keenly aware of the need to develop new relations among Irish people to transcend those old barriers that divided that community. These barriers are less evident on fete days when the whole local population crowds in for all the fun of the fair.

The rector acts as Anglican chaplain to the Belfield campus of University College Dublin.

Exterior of St Therese's.
PHOTO PETER COSTELLO

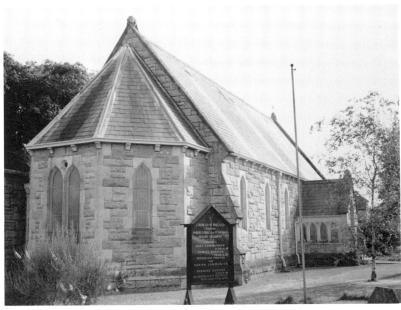

Exterior of St Thomas's, Mount Merrion.
PHOTO PETER COSTELLO

St Brigid's, Stillorgan

[CHURCH OF IRELAND]

Stillorgan is one of the old rural villages that have been swallowed up into Greater Dublin. In the eighteenth century the place was unremarkable except for the manor house of the Lord Allen which was the centre of much social life.

The church itself is of great interest as it remains largely unchanged from Georgian times, with a plain nave, and a side aisle added later along with an east window in early English gothic. The plain style is emphasised by the round-headed sash windows, with their gothic panes.

Holy Family, Kill-o'-the Grange

[ROMAN CATHOLIC]

In 1966 the old parish of Monkstown was extended to include another 220 families. But by 1972 it was found desirable to create yet another new parish in the higher part, and to build a new church at Baker's Corner.

Externally the new church with its brick curtain walls, cast concrete supports, and perspex skylights is chillingly modern. But the interior comes as a pleasant surprise. The light is filtered in from above to softly illuminate a church more in the style of a modern American evangelical church than anything else. The cruciform plan allows an openness which is added to by the galleries in the transepts. The pleasant atmosphere is enhanced by the plants which are grown in the corners.

Kill Church, Kill Lane

[CHURCH OF IRELAND]

The kill of the name is St Fintan's Church, just off Kill Lane, an early Celtic church with medieval additions, now in ruins. It is a National Monument.

The Anglican parish church which stands nearby was consecrated in July 1864, and is in an early Norman style on a small, intimate scale. The plainness of the work is relieved by the treatment of the apse and its windows. The bell-tower, with its reference to an early style, is also unusual.

The tower of St Brigid's, Stillorgan.
PHOTO PETER COSTELLO

Holy Family, Baker's Corner.
PHOTO PETER COSTELLO

Kill Church exterior.
PHOTO PETER COSTELLO

Holy Year Oratory, Cornelscourt

[ROMAN CATHOLIC]

To south Dubliners, Cornelscourt today means the great shopping complex. This was countryside up to twenty years ago, and the real fields still begin only a short distance away.

Tucked into one corner of the sprawling car park is the Holy Year Oratory. This extraordinary erection consists of three portable units which have been locked together to create two wings with pews for worshippers, and an entrance and sanctuary area in the middle unit. Curious though the chapel may sound, in fact it is an intimate and prayerful place. This is enhanced by the use of flowers and of Byzantine icons.

The little oratory combines the devotions so typical of rural Ireland with the needs of busy shoppers. It is not by any means a distinguished building, and serves as reminder that an attention to the qualities of a building may detract from a realisation that those who use it have their minds and hearts on higher things than bricks and mortar.

Our Lady of Perpetual Succour, Foxrock

[ROMAN CATHOLIC]

The Foxrock area, where Samuel Beckett was born in 1906, was a largely Edwardian development. The parish itself was created in 1917 from Ballybrack, along with Cabinteely which was hived off in turn in 1971 from Foxrock. The older church was St Brigid's in Cabinteely village, which dated from the mid-nineteenth century.

Our Lady's by contrast is a creation of the 1930s, being completed in 1935 (replacing a 'tin church' which had stood in Torquay Road). It is a granite building in a Byzantine Romanesque style, with a bell-tower on the northwest corner. The interior is painted largely white, with the capitals, Stations and window edges picked out in gold. The rounded apse and the side altars are backed by marbles in a most effective way. The dome of the apse is filled with a mosaic of the coronation of the Virgin. The red Roman tiles of the roof which echo the finish of many of the surrounding houses are effective here. Designed with restraint the church is pleasant and dignified in appearance, well-built and finished, with none of the touches of bad taste that affect some churches of the period.

Oratory at Cornelscourt.
PHOTO PETER COSTELLO

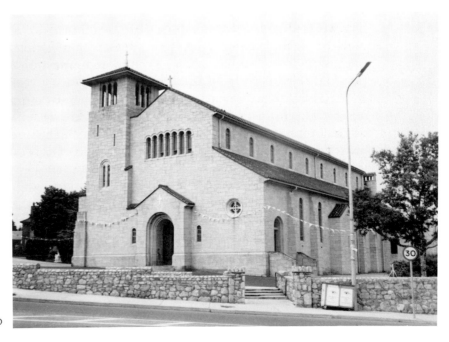

Our Lady, Foxrock.
PHOTO PETER COSTELLO

Tullow Church, Carrickmines

[CHURCH OF IRELAND]

Originally a rural parish, including Foxrock, Carrickmines and Brennanstown, Tullow is now a largely suburban parish with all that that implies. It lies towards the Dublin mountains behind Dun Laoghaire and Killiney. There were 220 families in 1969, nine moved out, but thirty have moved in: an indication of the population trend for Anglican churches in this part of Dublin. Tullow is an old Celtic name, from Tullagh na nEspuc, the Hill of the Bishops, which suggests there may have been a monastery there. A twelfth-century church in ruins remains.

The first church was in Cabinteely but had become ruinous by 1830. United then with Monkstown, Tullow became a separate parish again in 1860 and the building of a church at Carrickmines was begun. The church was consecrated on 9 April 1864 by Archbishop Trench. Designed by Welland and Gillespie at a cost of £1,600, the church was a plain rectangle with spire in a gothic style. The development of the area towards the end of the century brought salvation to what had been a not over-populated parish. The church was enlarged in 1904 by J. F. Fuller and further work was done in 1964.

Rathmichael Church, Rathmichael

[CHURCH OF IRELAND]

The parish is very ancient, for an old medieval church can be found off the Ballycorus Road. Rathmichael is also a prebend of St Patrick's Cathedral. For a long time it was united with Bray. In 1825 Kilternan was separated, and moves were made in Rathmichael to separate as well. The development of the country had brought new roads and new houses, increasing the population.

In 1860 work began on a new church in a Hiberno-Romanesque style. The architect was Sir Thomas Deane of Deane and Woodward, the distinguished Dublin firm. In the original plan there were no northern aisles or pillars, and the pew of the Domville family dominated the church. It was opened in 1864. A record of 1872 says there were thirteen Protestant gentlemen (supposedly with families) in the parish. By 1890 the church population was 300. Though untouched by the Troubles since 1958 Rathmichael has been in the position of having a growing population, rising school numbers and a vigorous parish life.

The church now has a northern aisle, open pews and a beamed wooden roof, and stained glass that is of some interest. Rathmichael is an unusual church in an unusual parish.

Tullow Church: the old fabric and the new porch.
PHOTO PETER COSTELLO

Rathmichael Church.
PHOTO PETER COSTELLO

St Anne's, Shankill

[ROMAN CATHOLIC]

Originally a chapel-of-ease to Ballybrack (which has an interesting church dating from 1863), St Anne's was erected in 1933 at the outer limit of the parish before reaching Bray.

It is an unexciting church in many ways, though solidly built in granite. The interior is severely plain, though not unattractive. There are signs that a certain amount of the finishing was skimped over for reasons of economy.

Now, with the development of the sea coast on either side of Corbawn Lane in the last ten years this has become a far more important church than its mother church, serving as it does a very mixed parish socially.

The church at Ballybrack is more interesting, however, from purely architectural point of view. It is very similar to the Anglican churches at Bray and Leeson Park, and without the grave of one of its priests, might be taken for a Church of Ireland church.

St Columbanus, Loughlinstown

[ROMAN CATHOLIC]

Constituted in 1982 from Ballybrack, Loughlinstown (again an area of mostly very recent development) only opened its church in 1988. Here at last the rising costs of building have caught up with the parishes, for after some difficulties over planning permission with Dun Laoghaire council, St Columbanus was finally consecrated.

It is a system-built church which is intended to be functional at a time of real need, rather than be a thing of aesthetic beauty. Nevertheless a pleasant enough structure has emerged from all the difficulties.

St Anne's in Shankill.
PHOTO PETER COSTELLO

St Columbanus' exterior.
PHOTO ROBERT ALLEN

Most Holy Redeemer, Bray

[ROMAN CATHOLIC]

Standing in a prominent position off the high street Holy Redeemer is a church which has been transformed in recent years.

The original church was a creation of Bray's years of development, and of its kind was a very attractive building with a dignified approach, in an unfussy gothic style. However, in the 1970s it was transformed by the erection of a new front façade in granite, with an enlarged porch and a new bell-tower with Romanesque features beside the transept. The original interior has been largely preserved, and its calm and undramatic nature contrasts with the extraordinary badness of what has been done to the front of the church. Here a passion for the new, which seems inappropriate in the context, has ruined what was a church of unpretentious beauty.

Christ Church with St Paul, Bray

[CHURCH OF IRELAND]

St Paul's was a church that antedated Bray's development as a resort, standing as it does on an ancient site just where the road to the south crosses the Dargle from Dublin to Wicklow. In Bray's heyday this was a popular church, in a town with a large resident and holiday Anglican population. But the change in the nature of the town, and the decline in the Anglican population overall, led to its closure (under protest from some) in the 1970s.

The design with its low nave and side aisles and squat square tower is a typical one of its period in the early part of the century. Closed up today, it looks out in decaying splendour on the hectic streets of new Bray.

The congregation has transferred to Christ Church, a gothic creation dating from 1863, with a landmark tower and spire from 1866. It stands on a hill in the southern part of the town, surrounded by houses standing in their own grounds developed in the 1870s to 1890s. This was the richer end of Bray, and retains to this day a great deal of elegant charm along deep tree-shaded roads.

The Celtic cross which stands in isolation in front of the church is not a war memorial, but commemorates a former incumbent. The war memorial is to be found in the porch, with the additional names from the Second World War on a stone set in to the ground at its foot. Tedious modernism is alien to the severe gravity of Christ Church.

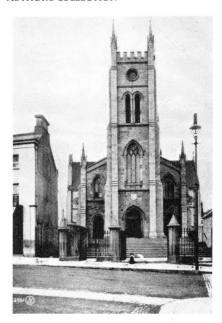

Holy Redeemer: the original façade about 1910.
AUTHOR'S COLLECTION

Holy Redeemer: the new façade and bell-tower.
PHOTO PETER COSTELLO

St Paul's closed to the world.
DRAWING BY PETER COSTELLO

The landmark spire of Christ Church.
PHOTO PETER COSTELLO

Miraculous Medal, Clonskeagh

[ROMAN CATHOLIC]

Though it was only made a separate parish in 1964, the church on Bird Avenue was built some ten years earlier. It belongs again to that hybrid style of Romanesque so common all over Dublin at this period. This is in most ways a more highly finished article. It was planned to cater for the immediate postwar development that had engulfed the area between Milltown and Dundrum, and was part of Donnybrook parish. The actual structure has given trouble in recent years, and signs of extensive damp are obvious on the internal walls.

Yet this church (by Felix Jones) is finely designed with a fine contrast between the brick-work and the mosaic-work, which is extensively used to wonderful effect. The Stations of the Cross are also in mosaic, with legends in English and Gaelic. The apse is filled with a mosaic of the Virgin. The Four Evangelists dominate the crossing. A very fine church of its period, its present problems may be compounded by the need for heat by modern congregations.

Holy Cross, Dundrum

[ROMAN CATHOLIC]

Dundrum church, with its distinctive sandstone façade, is among the most interesting in this area. It was built in 1877, and retains many features of its original creation. In 1953 it was extended by almost the same length again in a sensitive way which retains the old character, but provides more space in the church, and a hall underneath.

There had been a smaller church here dating from 1837 when the district was part of the extended parish of Booterstown. Today another church exists in Ballinteer nearby, thus continuing the breakup of the old parishes into smaller modern units.

Dundrum was a much sought-after place of residence because of its restorative air. It was a district of large houses in their own grounds, between which was the village crossroads of Dundrum where the church was built. There is a nativity window by Michael Healy, and the church retains in use sacred vessels of fine late Georgian design from the old church of 1837.

The Bird Avenue church.
PHOTO PETER COSTELLO

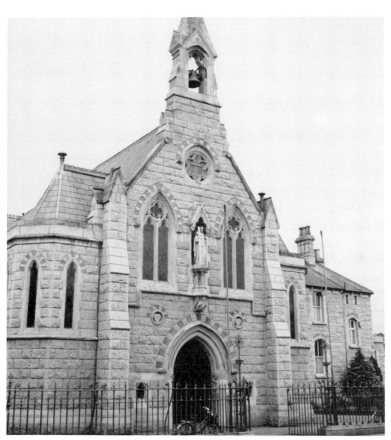

The front of Holy Cross church in Dundrum.
PHOTO PETER COSTELLO

Taney Church, Dundrum

[CHURCH OF IRELAND]

Taney Church was built in 1818, the original fabric being small. (It can still be seen where the north and south galleries join.) By 1827 it was found that repairs were needed but the problems were not solved until 1832. However, when in the 1860s the village of Dundrum came to be a sought-after place for health reasons, more improvements were thought desirable. The church was lucky in having a patron in Henry Roe to pay for these. The renovated church was rededicated in 1872.
St Nahi's, the old church for this neighbourhood, can still be visited on the hill off the Churchtown Road. It was restored by the Rev. Monk Gibbon, the father of the poet. A simple box with a bell cradle, it is an example of what many Irish churches, Catholic and Protestant, looked like in the seventeenth and eighteenth centuries. Regular services are still held here in continuation of a very ancient tradition.
Taney is the largest and most vigorous Church of Ireland parish in the greater Dublin area.

Whitechurch, Rathfarnham

[CHURCH OF IRELAND]

An example of John Semple's work, with his pinnacles, deep-set lancet windows, and plain façades, this is in the words of its rector 'a plain country church', and it has few remarkable features but the strength of its own basic architecture.
It stands in what had been a quarry on a prominence which gives the distinctive steeple a fine vista, especially from the road to the south. By the south gate is the tithe barn into which the rector of the day gathered his share of 'the first fruits'.
Originally part of Tallaght, the new parish was created and the church erected in 1825 on land bought from John La Touche of Marlay estate. This must have been one of Semple's first churches as architect to the Board of First Fruits.
In the graveyard which surrounds it is buried Annie M.P. Smithson, the ever-popular romantic novelist, who was for many years a district nurse in Rathfarnham. By the end of the 1960s repairs placed the parish in difficulties as there were so few parishioners, but today the congregation has risen sharply, and the rector is actually building a new school and employing 'a new curate'.

...aney Church with its 1818 cottages.
PHOTO PETER COSTELLO

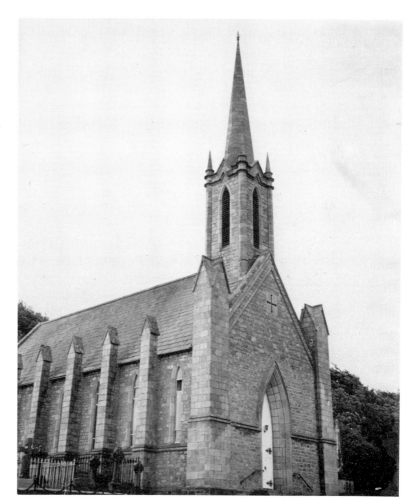

Whitechurch steeple from the graveyard.
PHOTO PETER COSTELLO

St Mark's Chapel, St Columba's College

[CHURCH OF IRELAND]

This little chapel has the distinction of being one of only two works in Ireland by William Butterfield, the high priest of the High Victorian style, and architect in ordinary to the Tractarian Movement and the Anglo-Catholics who followed them. St Columba's was part of the Tractarian flowering in Ireland, being founded by High Church enthusiasts in 1843 as a college without pupils. The pupils came and the school eventually moved to this site at Hollypark, outside Rathfarnham, in 1863. Here a temporary chapel of wood sufficed until this present one was erected by the architect's usual builders from Rugby in 1880.

This chapel is a lovely thing on the inside, aglow with golden stone. It is laid out in college fashion with the pews facing each other across the aisle. The period furnishings were provided as a gift by Magdalen College in Oxford. One of the fine windows is of St Mark with his symbolic lion. In 1958 the ante-chapel and screen were removed. In recent years to accommodate the increased number of both boys and girls at the college, changes have been made to the sanctuary and a gallery has been added, but these alterations have all been done in conformity with its creator's vision.

The college library treasures the *Mioseach*, an old Irish manuscript, authenticated by George Petrie as 'a genuine relic of your St Columba'.

The Assumption, Walkinstown

[ROMAN CATHOLIC]

By contrast to the Anglo-Catholicism of St Columba's, the Assumption is a church in the Irish Catholic tradition: a creation of the early 1950s, the parish being created in 1964. This is in a largely working-class area of Dublin, where what had been Terenure spread out over half a century to create Crumlin and Walkinstown. Nothing could be more in contrast with the intense nature of Butterfield's work than this utterly Roman, utterly public church. Romanesque in reference, it is built of dark red brick with granite footings and dressings. There are copper metal fittings and a slate roof. Standing on a large open site, surrounded on three sides by housing, it faces a range of school buildings, also in red brick with copper roofs, with which it forms a very harmonious and attractive ensemble. With this fine work on the part of the Church on the one hand, it is a pity that the Corporation housing on the other is not of better quality.

St Mark's Chapel in the grounds of St Columba's College.
PHOTO PETER COSTELLO

Exterior of the Assumption.
PHOTO PETER COSTELLO

St Maelruain, Tallaght

[CHURCH OF IRELAND]

In the nineteenth century Tallaght was a rural retreat, away from any urban hurly burly. The last two decades have changed all that, with the unparalleled development of the new town. However, right in the middle of the old village of Tallaght stands St Maelruain's church, on a very ancient site, though the church (as is so often the case) belongs to that intense period of Anglican building at the end of the Georgian era, being erected in 1829. However, by incorporating a medieval bell-tower it manages to still convey something of the old medieval aura. The architect was John Semple, and the church has the deep-set windows, pinnacles and solid arches typical of his work. The old church, which was built out from the tower, had become ruinous by 1825. Semple sited his rectangular church to one side on new ground.

The chancel was reconstructed and the furnishing improved in 1891. The gothic reredos, which is now such a prominent feature of the church, was installed then. In the 1960s the walls were stripped to the bare stone, which might not have appealed to Semple, though 'the dignified and beautiful simplicity' appeals to many.

The church is surrounded by a wild and curious graveyard in which many Catholics are buried. The parish population which was about fifty in mid-century, has risen to over 900 today.

St Mary's, Tallaght

[ROMAN CATHOLIC]

There are in the general Tallaght area some fourteen churches, most of them new, but St Mary's belongs (like St Maelruain's) to the earlier history of the area.

Though the site is historic enough, the monastery arriving in 1863, the church was completed only in 1886. It has been enlarged and modernised in recent years. The old chapel of the priory, the work of G.C. Ashlin in 1883, has been enlarged by the addition of a new nave making it the transept of the church. On the outside the 1969 extension (by Edward Brady, which won a European Heritage Award in 1975) is quite excellent, harmonising with the older building through the use of rustic limestone, and slender gothic arches in cast concrete. The interior is less successful.

St Maelruain's and its old graveyard.
PHOTO PETER COSTELLO

The new addition to the chapel of St Mary's.
PHOTO PETER COSTELLO

The interior transition from new to old at the sanctuary area.
PHOTO PETER COSTELLO

St Mary's, Lucan

[ROMAN CATHOLIC]

Lucan is an old village, and the church was once part of the ancient parish of Clondalkin, created in 1616. The parish church today is a very fine example of how an old structure can be renewed to meet the demands of a parish which has grown very rapidly in the last decade.

The early nineteenth-century church had been stripped of its plaster to reveal the rough limestone rubble stone-work, and has been used as a transept for a new church, with the altar on the crossing. The transition between the parts is handled more successfully than in the prizewinning church at Tallaght. The new part is simply built, with stock materials, but in the older part new wooden fittings for confessionals and so on echo the gothic style of the church.

St Andrew's, Lucan

[CHURCH OF IRELAND]

Though once a separate village, Lucan now is on the outer edge of Dublin, beyond which you pass into another county. The little village still has a certain charm, shared by this Anglican church. Now united with Leixlip (which is in Kildare) this parish has also found new numbers in recent years.

The church is typical of the early nineteenth century, and is comparable to the renovated Catholic church. The church fabric remains much as it was when the Church of Ireland was disestablished. Of interest too is the local Presbyterian church, dating from the 1870s, which has been enlarged recently and attractively remodelled inside to provide a small chapel and offices above. Again a piece of very fine work. The Methodists have found another solution for renewing the old: by removing the pews from their church they are able to give it over to nightly community use, putting out chairs for their own services on a Sunday.

At this outer edge of the city we can I think say farewell to the church alive in the faith of the villagers; and turn back to the lost churches of Dublin, where faith alone was not enough to keep them in existence.

Interior of St Mary's, Lucan village
PHOTO PETER COSTELLO

St Andrew's, Lucan.
PHOTO PETER COSTELLO

St Catherine's Church, Thomas Street

[EX CHURCH OF IRELAND]

A mong the most ancient of parish divisions in the city, the dedication is thought to have originated with a chapel belonging to the Abbey of St Thomas that stood before the Reformation on the site of the present church.

Called 'a sober classic' by John Harvey, the church was the creation of John Smyth (also responsible for the old St Thomas's) in 1760-69, and replaced an earlier and semi-ruinous church. The debt was not paid until 1774 so the planned spire was never put up.

The interior had interesting oak panelling and plaster-work, but nothing to rival the granite exterior, which has been called the finest classical façade in Dublin, 'a superbly virile composition' in Roman Doric, according to Maurice Craig.

In 1877 the church was restored by the architects Curdy and Mitchell, and in 1885 a major scheme, devised by J.F. Fuller, which replaced the old box pews with open ones, was undertaken. But what could not be repaired was the slow decline of the parishioners. There had been 600 in 1630; in 1943 the Rector recorded the loss of a third of his congregation in just one year.

The graveyard was closed for burials in 1894. The church itself was closed in September 1966. After deconsecration, the pews and the organ were taken away, though the latter was later restored through the work of a voluntary group, the Bell Tower Trust. Dublin Corporation, which took charge of the building in 1969, cleaned and restored the façade in 1975, and plans to make regular use of the building are now in the hands of the local Community Development Trust aided by the Bell Tower Trust and the Corporation.

James Malton's painting shows what it was like when it was (as a plaque now informs the world) the scene of Robert Emmet's execution in 1803, close to where the rebel band he was leading had butchered the humane judge Lord Kilwarden and his nephew. Among the plaques inside the church is a memorial to William Mylne who with 'uncommon zeal ... formed, enlarged and established on a perfect system the waterworks of Dublin'. Another is to the early nineteenth-century rector, the Rev. Whitelaw, who made immense efforts to relieve the distress in this area of Dublin brought about by the collapse of the weaving trade (essentially a Protestant trade) after the Act of Union.

St Catherine's Church as it was in 1793.
PAINTING BY JAMES MALTON. NATIONAL GALLERY OF IRELAND.

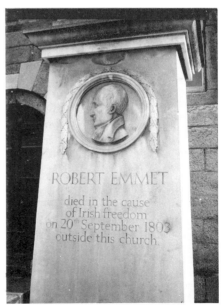

The memorial to Robert Emmet.
PHOTO PETER COSTELLO

The modern exterior.
PHOTO PETER COSTELLO

St Luke's, The Coombe

[EX CHURCH OF IRELAND]

Placed away in what some think of as an obscure part of Dublin, St Luke's in the Coombe was one of the most curious of Dublin churches.

The parish was created in 1707, but the church designed by Thomas Burgh and built by John Whimrey was erected only in 1714, being consecrated two years later.

Though the graveyard seems originally to have been a Huguenot place of burial, the French connection with St Luke's was slight, though of course many were settled in the Coombe as weavers. The Rev. Theophilius Broca, the minister at St Luke's, himself of French extraction, was a keen supporter of the developing industry in the 1740s. A decline in this trade in the early part of the nineteenth century left the neighbourhood impoverished.

The church was united again with that of St Nicholas-Without in 1862, when some enlargements were made to the simple original form of the church. The pulpit was placed in the centre, emphasising the evangelical nature of the services. Above the altar table was a device showing the veil of ignorance being pulled aside by the light of the Gospel.

Towards the end of the century the pulpit was moved aside. A feature of the church was a window in memory of Ellen Parkes, showing Christ stilling the storm, inserted above the altar. It was returned to the family in 1975. The church bell, with an inscription commemorating the Huguenots' arrival in 1685, was presented in 1903 to the church; it is now on display in St Patrick's.

Fronting the church was built an alms house, 'The Widow's House of the Parish'. This was closed in the early 1980s. The church itself became part of the St Patrick's group in 1974 and was closed for public worship in September 1975. It was then let to a commercial firm. It was intact, however, until a serious fire set by vandals destroyed the roof and interior on 26 October 1986. Now only the walls and traces of the old decoration survive.

St Luke's about 1818.
IRISH SCHOOL. NATIONAL GALLERY OF IRELAND

The Victorian porch of St Luke's.
DRAWING BY PETER COSTELLO

St James's, James's Street

[EX CHURCH OF IRELAND]

St James's was a medieval foundation, for a church was in existence in the twelfth century. It was attached by Archbishop Comyn to St Thomas's Abbey, the income being for the use of the poor. After the Reformation, it was united with the parishes of St John in Kilmainham and St Catherine to the east.

The old church quickly became a ruin, but was under repair by 1630. In 1707 a separate parish was recreated and a new church, 'a long, low and narrow building', was erected. This collapsed in 1761 and was again repaired.

The church that stands in James's Street today was the work of Joseph Welland, then architect to the Church Commissioners, in 1859. The Vestry after the Disestablishment was very Protestant in tone, and made frequent protests about the creeping ritualism they seem to have so easily detected in the life and furnishing of other churches. They went so far at to protest about the erection of a cross on the new rood screen in Christ Church, which was being restored by Henry Roe, the distiller, who was a resident in the parish. Roe made it clear that he felt he could not longer support St James's, the rector quickly withdrew the strong words of the Vestry, and no more protests appeared from their hands.

The population of the parish declined in this century, and the fabric of the church soon gave rise to concern. By 1941 the spire was in such a bad state that it had to be taken down after the Corporation became concerned about its dangerous condition. This was serious drain on very limited resources.

By 1956 it was suggested that the parish unite with St Catherine's and the church in James's Street be closed. This was done seven years later. The last service was held on Easter Sunday, 1963. The church was deconsecrated and sold for commercial use in 1967. It is now a warehouse for domestic light fittings. The old dedications continue at the church in Donore Avenue.

Behind the church, on a slope rolling down to the river, lies St James's graveyard. This had come into existence sometime in the sixteenth century. The last burial was in 1976. Many of those buried in the graveyard are Catholic, and families insisted on their rights to burial long after other graveyards were opened. Though the graveyard was cleaned and the graves recorded by a team of young people in the last few years, a recent visit found it once again overgrown and many of the stones overthrown and vandalised. Something more than local goodwill seems to be needed to preserve these relics of the city's history.

St James's church today.
PHOTO PETER COSTELLO

The sad condition of the graveyard behind the church.
PHOTO PETER COSTELLO

St Mary's, Mary Street

[EX CHURCH OF IRELAND]

S t Mary's is uniquely the only church in Dublin surviving from the seventeenth century. It was designed by Thomas Burgh and erected in 1697. It takes its name from the medieval Abbey of St Mary, the remains of which can be visited in nearby Meeting House Lane.

When it was built in the initial growth of Dublin under the Duke of Ormonde on the north bank of the river, it was in an important part of the city. But social change stranded it as fashion moved east and then south. It retained many of its original features such as its box pews and gallery. The organ which was the work of Renatus Harris was said to be the finest in Dublin.

The church contains the Ormonde family vault and a tablet commemorating members of the family. Lord Charlemont, the Volunteer Earl, was baptised here in 1728, Wolfe Tone in 1763, and more recently Sean O'Casey in 1880. John Wesley preached his first Irish sermon in this church in 1747. In the graveyard (now a public park) was buried Archibald Rowan Hamilton.

In 1986 the church was given over to the Greek Orthodox community who elevated it into a cathedral. Though it was not all that suitable for the Byzantine rite, they were pleased to use a building with such an ancient history. In the end of 1986, however, they were asked very suddenly to leave as the building was considered dangerous.

The church has a heavy external appearance, but inside is relieved by the fineness of its carving and decoration. Some of the figures carved on the organ case have been removed or vandalised by a puritan hand. It was the first galleried church to be built in Dublin, the gallery being supported on pillars, and in turn carrying the pillars supporting the vault of the ceiling. For nearly a century and a half many Dublin churches were built to the same pattern. The tower, as usual, was never finished.

It has not been used since 1986, and is beginning to decay. Here is a building with great potential for cultural use to which many tourists might be attracted, passing through a main shopping area of the city. With a little imagination much could be done to preserve St Mary's.

St Mary's as it appeared at the end of the eighteenth century.
NATIONAL GALLERY OF IRELAND

*Historical details fading on the church
notice board.*
PHOTO PETER COSTELLO

The church today, closed and boarded up in a busy part of the city.
PHOTO PETER COSTELLO

St Paul's, North King Street

[EX CHURCH OF IRELAND]

The church owes its origins to a division of the parish of St Michan's in 1697 into St Michan's, St Mary's and St Paul's. Here George Berkeley, the philosopher, was consecrated Bishop of Cloyne in May 1734. This is one of the churches where it is thought that Robert Emmet might have been buried after his execution in 1803. The first church was a galleried one, which was ruinous by 1821.

The church was rebuilt in the prevailing gothic style in 1821-4. It is not generally thought highly of in the roll-call of city churches.

It has a plain exterior. The nave is three bays long, with plain round-topped windows. Over the sanctuary there is a square tower with crenellations and gothic pinnacles. This too was an area of the city that went into social decline during the nineteenth century. During the events of Easter Week 1916 it was the scene of a serious affray in which many civilians were killed by British troops. The Protestant tradesmen on whom the church depended for its congregation vanished with the 1920s.

The church had some interesting items in it, including a famed painting of the Royal arms which came from the old St Paul's. A tablet in the church recorded the death of a Lt-Col. Browne 'North British Fuzileers, who was barbarously murdered by armed banditti in this city' in 1803.

The parish has been retained by the Church of Ireland, united first with All Saints Grangegorman, and later with three other inner-city parishes. The church itself has been closed and is now used as a youth employment training centre. In an area of great need this is at least serving the community in a real way which merely closing the doors and barring the windows would not have done. But lack of money is affecting the completion of the work recently commenced on the church to convert it.

Exterior of St Paul's today, with renovations under way.
PHOTO PETER COSTELLO

St George's, Hardwicke Place

[EX CHURCH OF IRELAND]

Standing on the higher ground to the north of the city, St George's is one of the city's most distinguished churches. There was an older St George's, built by Sir John Eccles for his tenants in 1714 and demolished in 1894, the black calp tower of which can still be seen at the bottom of Hill Street. But the tall graceful spire of this church is a landmark which dominates the neighbourhood around Dorset Street. It is the church from which Mr Bloom, busy with his breakfast in the kitchen of 7 Eccles Street, hears the bells sounding.

It was designed by that great architect of Dublin, Francis Johnston, who lived nearby and built between the years 1802 and 1813. As architect to the Board of Works Johnston made his mark on Dublin: beginning with Daly's Club in College Green and culminating in the General Post Office, but this church is undoubtedly his Dublin masterpiece.

The front façade is 92 feet wide with a portico of four fluted Ionic columns. It was a graceful but not a perfect building: he gave the nave a wide span of 65 feet, and as a result it nearly fell in 1836, only being saved by the erection of iron arches. The church was to cost £36,210 and money had been saved by buying shorter beams of wood than were needed. Johnston himself presented the bells to the church at a cost of £1,500.

In has a neo-Greek air, even to the inscription across the pediment. The spire, which he adapted from that of St Martin's-in-the-Fields, contrasts in style, rising a lofty 60 metres over the body of the church, a refined mixture of gothic inspiration with classical detail. When the church was built the interior was laid out more for preaching in the Presbyterian style, but was rearranged in about 1880 into the more usual Anglican form. It was a 'free church', with no pew rents, built on a site donated by the absentee landlord, the Earl of Blessington, the son of Luke Gardiner who built so much of this area.

St George's has now been closed and controversy raged in 1989 over what its future should be. As a cultural venue some felt it would be adversely affected by the area in which it stands: no-one's car would be safe.

The illustration is from one of the first photographs ever taken in Dublin by Fox Talbot's associate the Rev. Calvert Jones in the late 1840s. The fine Georgian houses which flank the church in his study have all been torn down and replaced by Corporation flats from the 1950s which already show terminal wear and tear. Undoubtedly this church should eventually become the focus for a major programme of urban renewal in this area of north Dublin.

St George's, Hardwicke Place, photographed by Rev. Calvert Jones about 1846.
COURTESY THE SCIENCE MUSEUM, LONDON

The Free Church, Great Charles Street
[EX CHURCH OF IRELAND]

Only a short distance away from both the Black Church and St George's, in Great Charles Street stands the Free Church. This was erected by the Methodists when the street itself was being built in 1800, and was designed by an architect named Robbins. The Methodists built their central church in Abbey Street in 1820, and no longer needed it. The landlord, however, refused to allow it to be sold for use as a Catholic church, so that it was bought by the Anglicans and reconsecrated in 1828, as a plaque above the door records.

This was a 'free church' in the sense that no pew rents were paid, and the incumbent depended on voluntary subscriptions from those attending his services. This was in keeping with the spirit of the evangelical movement.

The church stands at the head of Upper Rutland Street, which opens on to Summerhill. This whole area was then considered the best quarter of the city, a writer of 1820 remarking that 'the inhabitants of this parish are indeed almost exclusively of the upper ranks'. Among them was the artist, archaeologist and scholar George Petrie, who lived in No. 21 Great Charles Street. He later removed himself to Rathmines, as did many others of 'the upper ranks'. By the end of the century the whole area was in decline. Today parts of nearby Mountjoy Square are ruinous, there are blocks of flats in Great Charles Street and the Free Church is empty, the last service being held in 1988. The cost of repairing the church in the end proved too much for the Vestry.

It was placed on the market by the Representative Church Body with restrictions as to its use. It was bought by a charity to use as an education centre for Travellers. They plan to retain the features of the church, by using portable partitions to divide the space into work areas.

This firmly classical building, its plain granite façade topped by an undecorated pediment, speaks of the theological views of its builders. They would have approved of its renewal of life in the service of the community.

The Free Church in Great Charles Street.
PHOTO PETER COSTELLO

St Mary's Chapel-of-Ease (Black Church), St Mary's Place

[EX CHURCH OF IRELAND]

It is striking that as late as 1830 the Church of Ireland still felt the need to build a chapel-of-ease for an inner-city parish. Dublin, of course, had pushed out by then to the north along the road towards Phibsborough and Drumcondra, with the creation of many new streets. This was a largely fashionable area of the city, before the flight to the southside.

Popularly called the Black Church from the local black calp used to build it, St Mary's Chapel-of-Ease has what one writer calls 'a sombre and funeral effect'. Local legend had it that if you went twice round the Black Church the Devil would appear — a thought which provided the poet Austin Clarke, who was reared up here, with the title for his impressionistic memoirs of his childhood, dominated as they were by the effects of religion.

The man responsible for its creation was the remarkable Dublin architect for the Board of First Fruits, John Semple, and the church was finished in 1830. The exterior with its sharp needle-like pinnacles and the deep-set door and lancet windows is very typical of his work and unsurprising.

But the interior is truly extraordinary. The nave has literally no walls, the ceiling flowing to the ground in great parabolic curves. It is built of stepped stones (on the principle of the tomb at Mycenae) with only the very highest part being a true vault. The windows slope inwards with dizzying effect. Semple was always a man for arches in his churches, and here the whole church is one great arch. It was, so John Betjeman declared, his favourite Dublin church, and certainly as a structure it was a long way ahead of its time.

The photograph opposite is another in the series made by Fox Talbot's associate the Rev. Calvert Jones, and is one of the very first photographs or 'sun pictures' made in Dublin in the 1840s soon after the invention of photography. The view is taken from the south, and though the church is unaltered, the neighbourhood today is very different.

After it was built north Dublin began to decline. The church was closed and deconsecrated in 1962. Eventually it passed into the hands of the Corporation, who made some initial use of it for their traffic wardens and for displays but have let it out now to others for commercial purposes. What the future holds for this masterpiece of Dublin architecture remains in doubt. As Semple's only church in what was once Dublin proper it deserves the greatest care in its protection.

The Black Church photographed by the Rev. Calvert Jones in the 1840s.
COURTESY THE SCIENCE MUSEUM, LONDON

Trinity Church, Lower Gardiner Street
[EX CHURCH OF IRELAND]

Gardiner Street, which was begun about 1787, had by the turn of the century reached Beresford Place, erected then to face Gandon's Custom House. At the bottom of the street the Church of Ireland built Trinity Church in 1838. The architect was Frederick Darley.

Darley was related to the poet George Darley, and one of a family prominent not only in brewing (they were connected with the Guinnesses), but also with building and quarrying and speculative developments on the north side of the city. He designed the remarkable Palm House in the Botanic Gardens, the TCD Magnetic Observatory (now in Belfield), the Merchants Hall which faces the Metal Bridge, and the King's Inns Library.

In this catalogue, Trinity Church has a small place. The body of the church is built of black calp, while the classical façade is of yellow brick. It was among the largest churches in Dublin. But the social decay that crept over this area made it redundant. In the 1930s it was deconsecrated and bought by the Department of Social Welfare for use as a Labour Exchange. On weekdays the sight of the unemployed collecting their dole money here is a depressing one.

The former church now backs on to the Irish Life development in Abbey Street, which has transformed the area. But much of Gardiner Street still remains in open desolation.

The former Trinity Church in Gardiner Street, now a Labour Exchange.
PHOTO PETER COSTELLO

Quaker Meeting House, Eustace Street

[EX RELIGIOUS SOCIETY OF FRIENDS]

It should not be overlooked that the early history of the Quakers in Ireland was one fraught with hardship and persecution. The essence of founder George Fox's religious ideals was guidance by the inner light, with no hierarchy of priests or set of dogmas. They have no Baptism or Communion. Their views have always set the Friends apart, especially in Ireland. But they have contributed over the centuries in large measure to peace and social justice, and to the welfare of Dubliners.

Quakers first met in Dublin in 1655. This meeting house (which is now the theatre of the Irish Film Institute) was built in 1692. It then fronted on to Sycamore Alley, though an opening into Eustace Street was obtained in 1712. Various further additions were made, some with money from the sale of the Quaker burial ground at York Street on which the College of Surgeons now stands. The present entrance was created in 1859, when the premises were registered formally as the Meeting House, Eustace Street. Further alterations were made in 1877, with the old yard being roofed over to make a vestibule. The large meeting room, however, is virtually unchanged from the seventeenth century. Thomas Shillitoe, who made a temperance crusade visit to Ireland in 1811, wrote that a meeting in Eustace Street was 'like a feast of fat things after the storms we have endured'.

Indeed the gallery, which is such a feature of the hall, was essential to hold the crowds, Elizabeth Fry, the prison reformer, recording in 1827 that the throng was so large that 'we had difficulty in reaching the gallery. Hundreds went away disappointed'. The present gallery dates from the renovations of 1877, when steam heaters were also installed.

The Friends Institute was in Eustace Street from 1911 on, as well as the Friends Historical Library (a rich source of family and religious information). These have now been moved to Swanbrook House off Morehampton Road, where there is a long-established Quaker home for the elderly. There was also another meeting house in Meath Place, which was sold in 1986 and the offices moved to Swanbrook House.

The severe plainness of Quaker meeting houses, bare of decoration or devices, are extreme even in the Dissenting tradition, but for the Religious Society of Friends even the slightest ostentation has always been seen as a snare for virtue. Meetings are begun in silence, broken only when a particular Friend is moved by the Spirit to speak, read, or pray. All Quaker activities depend on individuals working together without leaders or superiors.

The Meeting House from the body of the hall.
PHOTO DIETER TANGAN. COURTESY FRIENDS HISTORICAL LIBRARY

The gallery, erected in 1877, to hold additional numbers.
PHOTO DIETER TANGAN. COURTESY FRIENDS HISTORICAL LIBRARY

St Andrew's Penal Chapel

[EX CHURCH OF IRELAND]

Catholics of an older generation were wont to make much of the grim days of the Penal Laws, and the dire effects these had on the practice of the faith. Yet as we have seen they have done little over the years to preserve any relics of this past. Parish priests have been more than anxious to pass on into bigger and better churches, and to throw off the integuments of the past.

At St Brendan's, Coolock, behind the new church there can be seen the pathetic boarded-up remains of the eighteenth-century chapel. It now has no role to fill, not even as a parish hall it would seem. At St Maur's in Rush the controversy rages over plans to demolish the old church, a charming thing in its way and much loved by most of the parish, in favour of a new enlarged church that would better meet the needs of the modern parish. So much for the past.

Even more striking was the fate of all that remains of one of the city's most historic churches. St Andrew's Catholic chapel stood on a site in Hawkins Street, where it had been opened about 1720 in what had been the stables to Lord Ely's house. It could not be readily seen from the road, as required by law, but seems from what we know of it (and from the sketch opposite made before 1818) to have been a well-appointed church. (This site now lies under Hawkins House.)

In 1738 a panic followed a collapse of the roof, and in 1750 a tall chimney stack fell into the chapel killing and injuring members of the congregation. After this the chapel was moved into what had been an old school house nearby facing on to Townsend Street, which remained in use until the opening of the new church in Westland Row in 1843. This was the chapel in which, as a plaque recorded until recently on the front of the building, Fr Mathew, the great temperance crusader of the early part of the nineteenth century, was baptised. For many Dubliners this was a striking and interesting association, worthy of reverent preservation.

Early in 1989 the house was demolished, except for a small part of the front façade shown in the photo, and the plaque removed for safe keeping to City Quay Church. A new office block will consume this historic site in due course.

Progress, we are told, cannot be resisted, but a city as ancient as Dublin, with so complex a history, should have some little respect for what has gone before. The Penal era of Ireland cannot be easily recalled in these more ecumenical days if its relics are swept away. These Penal chapels were a part of the ruthless treatment of dissenters by the authorities of the past. They are witness, in a city filled with denominations, of the religious freedom which dissent, including Roman Catholicism, has finally won.

The old Penal Chapel of St Andrew's parish.
NATIONAL GALLERY OF IRELAND

*The last wall of a Penal day chapel,
Townsend Street.*
PHOTO PETER COSTELLO

Bethesda Chapel, Dorset Street

[EX EVANGELICAL]

Standing on the corner of Granby Row, the chapel was built about 1789 by a William Smyth, who later attached to it an asylum for female orphans, who lived in the rooms above the chapel itself. The women sang at the services and the chapel was a popular place of worship.

As a chapel it was closed early in the present century and converted into a cinema in 1913. The orphanage which had declined into a slum was demolished. Though some structural changes were made in the 1960 when the cinema introduced Cinerama into Ireland, the building survives in a new form still and has more recently been converted into the Dublin Waxworks.

Molyneaux Chapel, Bride Street

[EX CHURCH OF IRELAND]

The complex of houses under the name of Molyneaux House dated back to 1711 when Thomas Molyneaux built the main house. Later it became a circus and a theatre. From 1815 to 1865 it was an asylum for the female blind, which later moved to Leeson Park, where a new church and home were built.

The amphitheatre created for the circus was converted into a chapel in 1862 and so survived until 1941 when it was sold to Jacob's factory as a recreation hall. The mansion itself was used as a refuge by the Salvation Army and was demolished in 1943.

In 1974, when Jacobs closed their biscuit factory, the chapel was bought by the architect Sam Stephenson, who refronted it and converted it into offices for Stephenson Gibney and Associates. On his removal to London it fell vacant. Behind the modernist brown brick façade which he created can still be seen the basic structure of the old chapel. As Mr Stephenson was responsible for so many of the buildings which have transformed the face of Dublin, this little chapel has now an added historical interest.

The Bethesda Chapel after conversion to a cinema.
PHOTO COURTESY FREDERICK O'DWYER

The façade of the old Molyneaux Chapel.

DRAWING BY PETER COSTELLO

The new façade of the old Molyneaux Chapel, built by Sam Stephenson.
PHOTO PETER COSTELLO

Ormond Quay Presbyterian Church

[EX PRESBYTERIAN CHURCH IN IRELAND]

The long runs of houses on the quays were the height of fashion when they were laid out, providing business men and professional men such as lawyers with homes as well as offices. Among the churches erected here was this elegant Presbyterian church dating from 1846, designed by E.P. Gribbon after an informal competition. The solid spikey towers recall Hawkesmoor's All Souls in Oxford. Among the long range of mainly Georgian houses on either side, the church stood out strikingly.

The church was for the Usher's Quay congregation, a union of several separate Presbyterian groups. In 1859 the church was extended to cater for a growing congregation, the building being pushed out to the rere over the site of a former school. The church was closed in 1938, the congregation uniting with the Scot's Church in Abbey Street. The building was later bought by a developer who proposed to erect a nine-storey block on the site. The church having been largely demolished nothing came of this scheme. However, in 1989 work was completed on new offices incorporating all that now remains of the gothic façade of the church.

Methodist Centenary Church, St Stephen's Green

(EX METHODIST CHURCH IN IRELAND)

The neo-classical building facing on to St Stephen's Green fronted a complex of buildings which included Wesley College. It was designed in 1843 by Isaac Farrell. The centenary was the foundation of the first Methodist society in 1739 by John Wesley. The interior of the church was destroyed by fire, so that only the granite façade and the portico survive. The church and the college were sold in 1972, the congregation moving to Leeson Park, the college to Ballinteer.

The building has been restructured completely to provide a banking hall and offices for the Smurfit Paribas Bank and other Smurfit concerns. The Victorian solidity of the building gives a certain grandeur to this temple of modern business enterprise.

Ormond Quay Presbyterian Church.
DRAWING BY PETER COSTELLO

New offices built on the remains of the church in 1989.
PHOTO PETER COSTELLO

The façade of Methodist Centenary Church today.
PHOTO PETER COSTELLO

Moravian Church, Kevin Street

[THE UNITED BRETHREN]

The Moravians, as the United Brethren are better known, originated during the Reformation in Bohemia. With a centre in the village of Kunwald they established a utopia based on the Sermon on the Mount. Breaking with Rome in 1467 they established the first of the independent Protestant churches. After 1620 the Moravians were driven out of Bohemia, but by then they were settled widely elsewhere.

The Brethren arrived in Ireland about 1740 where they were led by John La Trobe, who had been converted by the preaching of John Cennick. After he had preached in Dublin in 1746 a congregation emerged which was established in 1750. At its greatest extent the Moravian Church had eighteen churches and forty preaching houses in the country. They had an alms house in Whitefriars Street and a graveyard at Whitechurch.

In Dublin about 1760 they opened a church in Bishop Street which fronted on to Kevin Street. Though this is now a commercial concern the symbolic Lamb and Flag of the Moravians could be seen on the pediment until covered over recently. The Dublin Congregation ceased to exist at the end of December 1980.

Merrion Hall, Lower Merrion Street

[EX EVANGELICAL]

Though it has now been closed and sold for redevelopment, this building has been a remarkable feature of Dublin for over a century. The gospel halls that now remain are exactly that, halls in which the gospel is preached. The Merrion Hall, however, was a creation of the evangelical fervour of the late nineteenth century. It too was designed, by Alfred G. Jones in 1863, for preaching the gospel, with the pulpit in a central place on the first gallery level, while the seating rose in two levels supported on cast iron pillars in galleries to the front and side. The galleries were fronted with decorative cast iron. Its capacity was great, a couple of thousand at least.

Readers of *Ulysses* will recall that the advent of the Rev. Alexander J. Dowie, Restorer of the Church in Zion, to preach here is one of the lietmotifs of the novel. Alas, in life the colourful First Apostle of the church of Zion (later deposited by a flat-earther from his office for the sin of polygamy) never reached Dublin. But many others did, in the late nineteenth-century heyday of American evangelism. Dublin sees nothing like them today, and this very solid piece of architecture remains as a memorial to a fervour that found few followers here.

The former Moravian Church in Kevin Street.
PHOTO PETER COSTELLO

The Merrion Hall shortly after it closed.
PHOTO PETER COSTELLO

First Church of Christ, Scientist, Baggot Street
[EX CHRISTIAN SCIENCE]

The novel religions of America, the Latter Day Saints, Christian Science, Christadelphians, Seventh Day Adventists, are all represented in Dublin, and have found that minimum number of followers to keep their congregations alive. The one interesting building that came of their advent was the First Church of the Christian Scientists in Baggot Street.

This was a neo-classical temple on the site of what is now the Bord na Mona building, outside which the railings of the church still stand. The first branch was organised in Ireland in 1903, but it was not until 1925 that it was decided to build a church on a vacant site in Baggot Street. The foundation stone was laid in 1927 and the church opened in July 1928. The whole complex, which included reading rooms and offices, was completed in 1931 and dedicated in 1935, only after it was completely paid for. The total cost was £17,997, a huge sum of money then.

The building was sold and demolished in 1974, the Christian Scientists moving to an ordinary house in Herbert Park, one room of which has been fitted out in a simple style as a church for Sunday morning services. Though few in number, the Church is wealthy enough to maintain a presence in Dublin, and the doctrines of Mrs Eddy are of the kind that will always attract converts in all eras. Her message was the simple enough one of rejoicing in goodness and health, rather than living in fear of sin and illness.

Methodist Church, Charleston Road
[EX METHODIST CHURCH IN IRELAND]

Built at a time when this area was in expansion, Charleston Road Methodist Church was among the first churches to be deconsecrated. A very attractive building in old red sandstone, with cast iron railings, it has been tastefully converted into offices, now occupied by an insurance company.

Here is the kind of renewal of old churches which many would like to see done more often. (Century House in Harold's Cross nearby is another example.) But to the present writer there remains a loss to the community at large when a public building becomes a private one.

The exterior of the Baggot Street First Church of Christ Scientist.
COURTESY THE BOARD OF THE DUBLIN CHURCH

The present church in Herbert Park.
PHOTO PETER COSTELLO

Interior of the Baggot Street church.
COURTESY THE BOARD OF THE DUBLIN CHURCH

Charleston Road Methodist Church.
DRAWING BY PETER COSTELLO

Christ Church, Carysfort Avenue

[EX CHURCH OF IRELAND]

Now vanished to make room for the parking lot of a new office block, Christ Church went down fighting. The church was founded by Thomas Kelly as an independent bethel early in the last century. Kelly had been an Anglican but he was barred from the city pulpits by the archbishop, broke away from the Church and founded his own sect, the Kellyites. This was one of four chapels he built. After the demise of the sect the chapel was bought as a Trustee Church for the Anglicans.

The chapel formed the transepts of an enlarged church which functioned as a chapel-of-ease to Booterstown. However, this being an area too well supplied with churches, by the end of the 1950s it was clear to the church authorities that it would have to close. This was not a view shared by those who worshipped here. They took the Church Representative Body to court in March 1960, but lost their case. The church was closed, deconsecrated and demolished.

The Rev. Thomas Kelly has another memorial. He composed no less then 765 hymns, eight of which remain in the Church of Ireland Hymnal, including No. 514 'We've no Abiding city here'.

St Jude's, Inchicore Road

[EX CHURCH OF IRELAND]

Demolition also overtook St Jude's in 1988. On the road that leads away to the west of the city from Old Kilmainham, St Jude's when it was built was in an area of attractive middle-class development. On either side were large lodges standing in their own grounds. But the tide of history left it stranded.

The picture in the illustration is from a postcard made about 1906. On the back of it a young girl has written to her friend in America, 'This is the Church we go to it makes a pretty picture'.

And so it did, until recently. Now only the tower of the church remains, to become part of a development of eleven apartments. The stones have been carried away to Straffan in Kildare for re-use, and St Jude's is no more than a pious memory among a fading congregation.

The railings of Carysfort Church, now
enclosing a parking lot.
PHOTO PETER COSTELLO

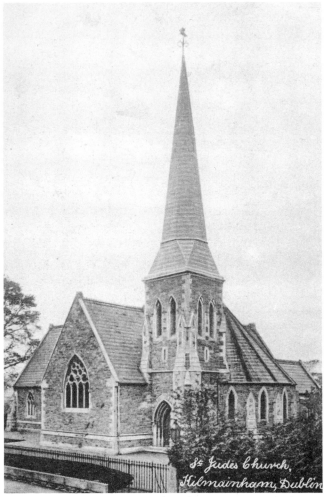

St Jude's, from a postcard of 1906.
AUTHOR'S COLLECTION

St Jude's today: a pile of rubble and a derelict church hall of iron.
PHOTO PETER COSTELLO

St Doulagh's Church, Balgriffin

[CHURCH OF IRELAND]

Among the most remarkable of Dublin churches is St Doulagh's (also called St Doulough's). The dedication was once attached to a lost church within the old city; this church dates from perhaps the twelfth century. It is strongly built in solid stone, with walls three feet thick, and has weathered the centuries remarkably well. The battlemented tower dates from the fifteenth century. The original building, with a double roof, consists of several vaulted rooms, one above another and connected by stairs, part of the old monastic settlement to which various names have been given. One small niche in the thickness of the wall at the head of the second flight of steps is said to have been the penitential bed of the saint, and upper chamber a hermit's cell. Nearby, though outside the old wall which surrounds the church, is the holy well of the Blessed Virgin, rising in a circular stone base over which has been erected an octagonal canopy. This was decorated in the seventeenth century with paintings by Patrick Fagan of Feltrim. The pictures showed the Descent of the Holy Spirit, with the saints Patrick, Brigid and Columcille, and St Duilech himself in the robes of a hermit. The shrine was completed with a Latin poem in praise of the saint and the virtues of the well. The paintings were destroyed by Sir Richard Bulkeley and his troops returning from the battle of the Boyne. An annual pattern was held here until it was suppressed by the clergy in the last century.

In the early 1860s a committee headed by Lord Talbot de Malahide raised money for the renewal of the church. An addition was begun in 1863 in gothic Revival style by W.H. Lynn, the Belfast architect, which manages to blend into the old fabric very well. It was blessed and reconsecrated by Archbishop Trench in 1865.

This church is still used for services of the Church of Ireland. St Doulagh's thus retains a revived connection with the earliest days of Christianity in Dublin: the ancient church has found a new life of worship. This would be the ideal for all the older churches of Dublin, and the continuity of faith would preserve them from the indifference of the age. But if that is not to be, let us hope that they are at least preserved from the desecrating hands of the descendants of Richard Bulkeley, and find some form of new life in the community compatible with their sacred character.

Renovated exterior of St Doulagh's.
PHOTO PETER COSTELLO

Further Reading

Anon, *Illustrated Guide to Dublin with Notes on its History, Antiquities and Industries*, Dublin: Messenger Office 1907.

Carey, F.F. [Benin], *Catholic Dublin: an ecclesiastical guide*, Dublin: Trinity Press 1932.

Champneys, Arthur, *Irish Ecclesiastical Architecture*, Dublin 1910.

Chart, D.A., *Dublin*, rev. ed., London: Dent 1932.

Cosgrave, Dillon, *North Dublin, City and Environs*, Dublin: CTSI 1909.

Craig, Maurice, *Dublin, 1660-1860*, London: Cresset Press 1952.

Crawford, John, *Around the Churches*, Dublin 1988.

Crawford, John, *Within the Walls: the story of St Audoen's Church, Cornmarket, Dublin*, Dublin 1986.

Donnelly, Nicholas, *Roman Catholicism: state and condition of RC chapels in Dublin, both secular and regular, A.D. 1749*, Dublin: CTSI 1910.

Donnelly, Nicholas, *Short Histories of Dublin Parishes*, Blackrock: Carraig Chapbooks, n.d.

Gills Guide to Catholic Dublin, Dublin: M.H. Gill and Son 1932.

Harvey, John, *Dublin: a study in environment*, London: Batsford 1949.

Hurley, Richard and Cantwell, Wilfrid, *Contemporary Irish Church Architecture*, Dublin: Gill and Macmillan 1985.

Hyman, Louis, *The Jews in Ireland*, Shannon: Irish University Press 1972.

Jackson, Victor, *St Patrick's Cathedral*, Dublin: Easons 1982.

Joyce, Weston St J., *The Neighbourhood of Dublin*, Dublin: M.H. Gill and Son 1921.

Kane, Eileen, 'John Henry Newman's Catholic University Church in Dublin', *Studies*, Summer-Autumn 1977.

Kennedy, T.P., 'Church Building' (*A History of Irish Catholicism*, vol. 5, ch. 8) Dublin: Gill and Macmillan 1970.

McDermott, Matthew J., *Dublin's Architectural Development 1800-1925*, Dublin: Tulcamac 1988.

Mac Giolla Phadraig, Brian, *History of Terenure*, Dublin: Veritas 1954.

Milne, Kenneth, *S. Bartholomew's: a history of the Dublin parish*, Dublin: Allen Figgis 1963

O'Donnell, E.E., *The Annals of Dublin — Fair City*, Dublin: Wolfhound Press 1987.

O'Dwyer, Frederick, *Lost Dublin*, Dublin: Gill and Macmillan 1981.

Parish Guide to the Archdiocese of Dublin, Dublin: Irish Church Publications 1968.

Poyntz, S.G., *St Ann's, the Church in the Heart of the City*, Dublin 1976.

Purcell, Mary, *Dublin's Pro-Cathedral*, Dublin 1975.

Sheehy, Jeanne, *J.J. McCarthy and the Gothic Revival in Ireland*, Belfast: Ulster Architectural Heritage Society 1977

Stokes, A.E., *Christ Church Cathedral*, Dublin: Easons 1983.

Wheeler, H.A. and Craig, Maurice, *The Dublin Churches of the Church of Ireland*, Dublin: APCK 1948.

Acknowledgments

I am very grateful to all those parish priests, heads of houses, rectors, ministers, pastors and lay persons who so generously helped, often at short notice, with gathering the facts and impressions for this book.

I am also very grateful to Miss Olive Daly for her heroic assistance at the wheel of her car in touring greater Dublin from north to south, often in bad weather. Her company made the whole task pleasanter. I am indebted to Patrick Costello for the use of his camera; and to Damien Maddock, of DM Prints, who has made pictures out of my snapshots.

I am also grateful to the as always more than helpful staff of the National Gallery, the National Library, the Irish Architectural Archive, and the Central Catholic Library. For the things I should have found out and didn't I have only myself to thank.

For their help or assistance on particular points I am grateful to Freddy O'Dwyer, Ninian Faulkiner, Mrs D.E. Jenkinson, Mrs Pearl Lamb, Robert Allen, and Fr Noel Madden V.F.

This book had its origins in an exhibition for the Millennium which was mounted at the Central Catholic Library in the summer of 1988, which was rather grandly entitled 'A Thousand Years of Christian Dublin'. That exhibition was deeply indebted to Dr Noel Kissane, the Education Officer of the National Library of Ireland, without whose very practical aid it could not have got beyond being a mere concept. I worked on that exhibition with Miss Nicole Arnould, the Assistant Librarian, and my heartfelt thanks are due to her for all her trials in dealing with authors.

My family too has borne patiently with this project. They should be content that at least it is out of the way quickly.

Finally, a word of thanks to the designers and builders of these churches, and to those who paid to have the work done, from Cardinal Cullen and Henry Roe to the children who put their pennies in the collection boxes. They have all helped not only to make this book, but to create the city of Dublin.

Peter Costello
Dublin 1989

Index

BRANDEIS UNIVERSITY
DALLAS
TEXAS